D0776881

OLD DOGS, NEW TRICKS

WARREN BENNIS

Ordering Information:
Individual Sales: Executive Excellence Publishing products are available through most bookstores. They can also be ordered directly from Executive Excellence Publishing at the address below.

Quantity sales: Executive Excellence Publishing products are available at special quantity discounts when purchased in bulk by corporations, associations, libraries, and others, or for college textbook/course adoptions. Please write to the address below or call Executive Excellence Publishing at 1-800-304-9782.

Orders for U.S. and Canadian trade bookstores and wholesalers: Executive Excellence Publishing books and audio tapes are available to the trade through LPC Group/Login Trade. Please contact LPC at 644 South Clark Street, Suite 2000; Chicago, IL 60605, or call 1-800-626-4330.

For permission requests, contact the publisher at:

Executive Excellence Publishing
1344 East 1120 South
Provo, UT 84606
phone: 1-801-375-4060
fax: 1-801-377-5960
www.eep.com

Printed in the United States of America
10 9 8 7 6 5 4 3 2   04 03 02 01 00 99
ISBN: 1-890009-34-2

Cover design by Joe McGovern
Cover illustration by Andrew Knaupp
Printed by Publisher Press

DEDICATION

For my wondrous tricksters,

Kate, John, and Will.

CONTENTS

A Tribute to Warren Bennis . . . One old dog who keeps learning

by Ken Shelton

Many "old dog" managers and leaders were sorry folks who could neither enjoy the use of a thing nor let anyone else enjoy it. They lived a "dog's life," feeling fairly wretched and miserable, engaging in "dog-eat-dog" (ruthless and savage) competition, and becoming "dog tired." They were then considered over the hill, done in, used up, and then "dog gone."

But if we throw our maturing management and our organizations "to the dogs," we inevitably throw away as useless something that may have tremendous value; if we let things "go to the dogs," they tend to deteriorate or fall to pieces fast; and if we "let sleeping dogs lie," we try to let well enough alone, not disturbing things but leaving them as they are for fear of something worse.

Bennis rejects these old adages and archetypes, advising us to "put on the dog," becoming more elegant in simplicity and wealthy in wisdom and self-worth. He shows us again that "every dog has its day," meaning that something fortunate happens to everyone at one time or another, even later in life, as we enter a "dog's age" (living and working a comparatively long time) and toy with a poodle of an idea—never retiring.

Bennis himself is a living example of the exemplary leader—a distinguished old dog who, both by choice and by chance, has learned many new tricks.

As valuable as he might be as a role model, he is even more valuable as the voice of leadership today. He both calls the play by play, and adds color commentary.

The concept for this book came about one day when it occurred to me that Warren Bennis, while being of the "old dog" WWII generation, knows personally just about every "who's who" leader of his day. He bridges not one but three generations—always in style, no gaps or yaps, only distilled wisdom. And so who better than Bennis to say what both old and young dogs alike must do in their days on the watch to learn new tricks and lead us through the new millennium.

A Tribute to Old Dogs

by Warren Bennis

In today's complex world of work, people in every position and organization, and especially senior managers and executives (the "old dogs"), must learn to work as great groups and creative coalitions rather than rely solely on lone rangers, solitary wolves, charismatic leaders, and John Wayne mavericks.

The "lucky dogs" are those who learn early that the "dog's life" of leadership need not be low and contemptible, that their "bark" can be better than bit parts and sound bites, as they learn the relatively "new tricks" of collaboration and transformation.

The truth for many leaders is simply this: either learn new tricks, or be gone—even dog-gone!

Frankly, I've been fairly impressed that so many senior executives and seasoned managers have learned not only difficult new technology tricks but more importantly new styles and mind-sets. Some have had to shed old prejudices, biases, and habits and grow new perspectives and leadership capabilities.

Unfortunately, I must also say that many senior executives have remained rather insulated, isolated, and even protected from learning new tricks. The old way, their way, is not only the best way, it's the only way—other than the highway.

When leaders become static, they often become autocratic. That all-too-familiar style sends many followers to the exits, looking, often in vain, for real leadership: somebody or something worthy of their loyalty and trust.

Today, leadership is more important than ever before. In Great Britain, one survey noted that 65 percent of executives believe there is a shortage of high-caliber leaders. *Business Week* once had a cover story: "Wanted: A Good CEO." And *The Financial Times* ran an article: "Desperately Seeking CEOs."

EARLY LESSONS IN LEADERSHIP

Most of us gain our early lessons of leadership, both good and bad, from our childhoods. I grew up in a family of three boys. My older brothers, 10 years older than I am, are identical twins, and to this day they're impossible to tell apart. We gave them a surprise birthday party on their 82nd birthday, and I had to squint to see who was who.

Growing up in that family was, to say the least, very interesting. When I was about seven years old, I began noticing the pattern of leadership and followership. One of my brothers seemed to have the right stuff. Whatever he suggested, my friends and I would follow automatically—going to a game, playing a sport, doing a picnic, going to a movie, ditching school—whatever it was, we followed; whereas when his twin, his double, suggested the same thing, we curiously declined. Nothing happened. It was like acoustical dead space.

I began wondering, "What is the difference between people who seem to have the capacity to enroll people in their vision, and those who don't?"

Most of my life I've been curious about leadership. I joined the army and entered World War II as a 19-year-old kid, playing for mortal stakes, and I observed different leaders there. But maybe my best learning experience was being a university president. That was a daunting experience for me, and I can't claim I was a great success at it. But I learned a lot.

I have spent much time over the past 20 years up close with leaders, trying to learn what they do, what their direct reports think of them, and gaining a prismatic view to tease out of them or to discern their characteristics, and identify a cluster of competencies or qualities that exemplary leaders manifest.

Beyond qualities, however, I've also looked for actions and learning experiences—what leaders do to rise to the top and what they must learn and do to stay there. Remarkably, many old dogs have an amazing regenerative capacity for learning new skills and mastering new tricks. Even when they are thought by some to be washed up, over the hill, all bark and no bite, the best of them reinvent themselves and come back strong to lead their organizations to new highs.

Learning the new tricks in this book will qualify you as one of these exemplary leaders.

INTRODUCTION

Most organizations use some criteria to evaluate people in terms of their leadership capacity. Sometimes this criteria is soft, unwritten and very subjective, even highly political. As one second-generation leader, the son of the company founder, said about his early promotion to the position of executive vice president, "A Harvard MBA has nothing over nepotism."

A more objective set of criteria to determine whether people move up, stay where they are, or get derailed might include the following seven: (1) technical competence, (2) people skills, (3) conceptual skills (the capacity to think big and make connections), (4) the ability to track and record results, (5) people taste (do they choose people well?), (6) judgment (the capacity to make important decisions with imperfect data in a short time), and (7) character (what the person is really like).

I see such criteria as hygiene factors—they are necessary to gain the top positions but insufficient to perform well in them.

THREE SECTIONS

When I look back over the last 20 years of studying leadership competencies, I start with the question: "What do people want and need?" I think that what people want from their leaders is represented well in the three sections of this book:

Section I: A sense of purpose or meaning. Above all, leaders must provide purpose to enable authentic human relationships, along with the optimism that things will work out well, a confidence that one can influence the circumstances of one's life, an expectation of a future good.

Section II: A sense of belonging, community, team, or group. People don't want to feel isolated, alone and lonely, to face the challenges at work. They want to feel valued and supported as a member of a great group or dynamic team.

Section III: A sense of power, involvement, connection, alliance. Leaders must share power and broker involvement and participation and make sure that alliances are strong and mutually rewarding.

As you learn and apply the tricks of the new trade, you will have more treats to pass around.

SECTION 1

Tricks of the New Trade

The new trade is all about vision, meaning, purpose, and trust—and what it takes to maintain these essential elements in modern organizations.

When trust is in short supply, the organization experiences something akin to a drought or famine. It's as if the water, food, air, or lifeblood is gone. It's hard to breathe easily. Everything is a bit forced. Nothing seems to flow easily or naturally.

The tricks in this section have often been referred to as the "soft side" of the management, but in my experience the authentic leaders who perform these tricks well are anything but soft. They may be tender-hearted, but they are first and foremost tough-minded in their pursuit of the desired vision state.

TRICK #1

Follow Your Spirit

Once more unto the breach, dear friends, once more.
Follow your spirit, and upon this charge cry "God for
Harry, England, and Saint George!"
———William Shakespeare

What is it that makes us go riding unto the breach—following even those leaders who don't have Will Shakespeare writing their speeches? Some would argue that the answer is charisma—and you either have it or you don't.

I don't think it's that simple. I've spent the last 20 years observing and talking with leaders worldwide. In the course of my study, I've met many leaders who couldn't be described as charismatic by any sort of rhetorical stretch, but they nevertheless managed to inspire an enviable trust and loyalty in their coworkers. And through their abilities to get people on their side, they were able to make real their guiding visions.

These are men and women who work with their hearts, not just their heads; with the right, creative side of their brain, not just the left, logical side. They are comfortable with imagery, symbolism, metaphor, logo, brand, and design. They find a metaphor that embodies their vision. For Charles Darwin, the fecund metaphor was a branching tree of evolution on which he could trace the rise and fate of various species. William James viewed mental processes as a stream or river. John Locke focused on the falconer, whose release of a bird symbolized his "own emerging view of the creative process"—that is, the quest for human knowledge.

Having had my own bouts with illness, I have had to face the reality of my own mortality. I have come to see life metaphorically: as an hourglass filled with grains of sand. I also see that the marginal utility of each grain of sand is more precious than I previously imagined. Each day is more exciting and interesting, perhaps because there are fewer of them ahead.

I sometimes wonder why some senior executives seem to think they are immortal, as evidenced by their lack of succession planning. Why must the succession of leaders routinely cause such consternation in organizations?

I must say that I am opposed totally to the idea of retirement. I think we can use "old dogs" in new and better ways than in the past. Personally, at age 74, I'm working just as hard as I ever have in my life, and with more focus and passion around what I believe to be my mission. Indeed, in these golden years, the life of the spirit becomes as real as the life of the body.

This is not to say that I think it's good for senior people to stay in their jobs forever. We do need to give the younger generation a chance. I've always advocated a five-to-seven-year rule. I think a person should change jobs every five to seven years. Such movement forces one to keep learning new tricks, even new trades.

I think you've got to have a sense of wonder and hope. Leaders are purveyors of hope who suspend disbelief in their groups. They don't know this can't be done. Real leaders transform minutia into meaning. We are all hungry spirits, looking for meaning at work and wherever else we can find it. And any leader who can dangle before us a dream usually gets our attention and our talents to make that dream a reality.

I spell out four competencies in leaders: (1) attention to vision, providing people with a bridge to the future; (2) giving meaning to that vision through communication; (3) building trust, the lubrication that makes organizations function; and (4) the search for self-knowledge and self-regard. These same four competencies must also be found in followers.

I'm sometimes surprised by the universal acceptance of these basic competencies. Once I addressed an audience in Brussels, then spoke to 600 managers in Newcastle, Great Britain. To my amazement, what I had to say about the four competencies resonated with the English and the Europeans. And what I'm saying, basically, is that leadership is all about character. There are, of course, cultural nuances to character. In Asia, for example, your resume may not be as important as your relationships, your web of connections. But in most parts of the world, we try to base promotion not only on merit (competency) but also morals (character).

In my work with leaders, I emphasize the importance of character. Integrity is an essential ingredient in successful leaders as well as in great organizations. I see a "tripod" of leadership: one leg is ambition or drive; one is competence or expertise; and the third leg is integrity or moral fabric. Imagine someone with just ambition and you get a demagogue. Imagine someone with just competence, and you get a leader who destroys the soul of the organization.

In times of turbulence and change, people often pick a leader who has ambition and competence, but little integrity. Ultimately those leaders fail—and the price their followers pay is enormous. If history tells us anything about leaders it is this: in picking a leader, insist on integrity.

The need for "value-based leadership" is not new. Leaders must possess a moral compass, correlate their vision and values, and do the right thing in the moment of truth. Leadership means more than increasing the wealth of shareholders.

Create the situation. When you follow your spirit, you are more likely to create the situation, not just react to it. Let me contrast the views of Leo Tolstoy, the Russian novelist, with those of Thomas Carlyle, the British historian. Tolstoy believed that men were always the effect, rather than the cause, of events. Events have their own historical force and, at best, a leader can guide the way. This viewpoint of situationalism is opposite that of Carlyle, who believed that history is a succession of biographies. Every institution is the "length and breadth of one great man." Personally, I lean toward Carlyle's view and believe that great leaders create the situation. And not necessarily where the situation is currently but where it is headed. An effective leader sees through the fog of reality to interpret events and make sense of the blurring and ambiguous complexity. But, even if you have the best vision in the world, if you can't generate trust, it doesn't matter. And it's not just trust in an abstract sense. It's the ability to connect with people in their hearts and souls, not just in their heads.

The CEO of a large transportation firm once said to me, "I run a company where I think we know where the trends are going to be, but I can't get the union, the work force, or anybody to actually go with me on that vision." He talked in very negative terms about his overall operation, but never acknowledged the fact that the people in the firm do not trust him. They see him as a "revolving SOB," an SOB regardless of the angle from which they look at him. So he has the vision and the ability to see through the fog of reality, but he can't get the people to follow him.

He reminds me of Glendower, the Scottish seer in Shakespeare's Henry IV, who boasts, "I can call forth the spirits from the vasty deep." And Hotspur deflates him by responding, "Well, so can I. So can any man; but will they come when you call them?"

This type of spiritual leadership requires not just interpreting and envisioning the future, but creating meaning for people, articulating values that make sense to them, and maintaining trust in the system.

I'm not saying that situations are not important. The effective leader has to size up the situation, forge a new path to the future, have a message and vision that have meaning to people. Without that, you can call for the spirits from the vasty deep forever, but they won't come.

The challenge today, as always, is to create and maintain trust, especially in this era of downsizing. If leaders can't establish trust, then participation and empowerment will be cynical relics of a distopian nightmare. The problem is squarely in the hands of leaders, and it's a moral and spiritual challenge that will confront us well into the next century.

TRICK #2

Start with Purpose

People need meaningful purpose. That's why we live. With a shared purpose, we can achieve anything. All the leaders I know have a strongly defined sense of purpose. And when you have an organization where people are aligned behind a clearly defined vision and purpose, you get a powerful organization. I can't exaggerate the significance of a strong determination to achieve a goal—a conviction, a passion, even a skewed distortion of reality that focuses on a particular point of view. And the leader has to express that determination or purpose in various ways. Max De Pree, the former CEO of Herman Miller, once said, "The first task of a leader is to help define reality." That's another way of talking about purpose. Without a sense of alignment behind a purpose, the organization will be in trouble, because the opposite of having purpose is to drift aimlessly.

And it can't be any old purpose if it is to galvanize and energize and enthrall people. It has to have meaning and resonance. And there's no reason why a persuasive point of view can't be an ethical one. Do you want a more ethical organization and society? Then exercise moral leadership when making decisions, and be a forceful, committed advocate for ethics. Your deeply held purpose or point of view may well carry the day.

Purpose is a small word, two syllables, but it contains three major dimensions: passion, perspective, and meaning.

• *Passion.* I have never met a great leader who wasn't passionate. By *passionate,* I don't mean they have to shout and be charismatic. Many leaders are rather soft-spoken, but when you hear them talk, you sense their passion.

One of my great American heroes is Abraham Lincoln, and he once said, "I must keep some standard of conviction fixed within myself." Another of my heroes is Margaret Thatcher. Whether you agree with Margaret's policies or not, you must agree that she has extraordinary passion, conviction, and compelling beliefs. And it's interesting that her successor, John Major, a very decent person all-around, lost the last election by a landslide to Tony Blair, the new labor party leader, largely because he lacked conviction and passion. The same might be said of George Bush in his race against Bill Clinton.

Often passion is associated with a strong point of view. Michael Eisner once told me, as we walked around the feature animation studios at Disney Studios, that Disney didn't have a "vision statement" but rather a strong "point of view" about the Disney culture. "When we have our president's meeting every week, we often make multi-million dollar decisions about movies and theme parks and products. It's amazing to me that the person with the strong point of view almost always wins the day. Around here, a strong P.O.V. is worth at least 80 I.Q. points." Again, what he's talking about is passion and compelling belief.

Speaking on the importance of maintaining perspective, Michael Eisner notes: "One danger of fast growth is that a company can lose its focus, forget its mission, and take its eye off its core competency. Not only is rapid growth a problem but success, unless properly handled, can be toxic."

So, how can you grow and avoid the pitfalls? How can you manage a company like Disney, whose principal asset is creativity, and keep it young and vibrant without losing upward trajectory or your sense of adventure? Eisner says, "We must be open to new ideas from every source and create an atmosphere in which people feel safe to fail. Otherwise, potentially brilliant ideas are never shared. Once you have the best ideas on the table, you can then follow through and execute them."

• *Perspective.* When you have perspective, you have a helicopter point of view. When you have perspective, you gain discernment, insight, and foresight. You have a sense of the past, present, and future. The question today is, what happens after what happens next? I often tell people, "Yes, you understand the situation, but what you don't understand is that the situation has changed." This is why leading people in today's world is so difficult, confusing, turbulent, vexing, and perplexing. But it's also exhilarating, exciting, and thrilling.

Competitive edge comes from an ability to live in the fog of reality and still make rapid, excellent interpretations of where the world is at this moment and where it's headed. Bob Galvin, vice-chairman of the Motorola board and a terrific leader, has such ability. His father started the business back in the 1920s with the following insight: "Automobiles are now affordable by the middle class. Radios are now becoming one of the dominant forms of communication. Why don't we have radios in cars? We can call them Motorola." It sounds obvious, doesn't it? Before World War II, he realized that in war, communication is a basic issue. "How does a platoon leader on the front line communicate with the artillery people? Well, you need a walkie. So we developed the walkie-talkie." That's anticipation. That's foresight. That's vision. I don't know how you teach that trait, but successful executives have it.

The late Roberto Goizueta, past chairman of Coca-Cola, said it beautifully: "If you think you can run your business in the next 10 years the way you've run it in the last 10 years, you're crazy. To succeed in the next decade, you'll have to disturb the present." He's right, of course. If you look at the Fortune 500 every 10 years, you will see that the average attrition rate is about 40 percent.

• *Meaning.* Another exemplary leader is Robert Haas, CEO of Levi Strauss. He once said, "The most visible differences between the corporation of the future and its present-day counterpart will not be the products they make or the equipment they use, but who will be working, why they will be working, and what work will mean to them."

Motorola has a "personal dignity" program that suggests that every person should have a "substantive, meaningful job that contributes to the success of Motorola." One of Galvin's ideas is that everybody at Motorola should leave a legacy.

I would define *meaning* as information endowed with purpose and relevance. We are all wanting to make a contribution. We all are seeking meaning of one kind or another in our lives, and we need it at work.

How important is meaning to Michael Eisner and Disney? Says Eisner: "I'm passionate about what I do because the most successful export is the so-called American dream. You find meaning and produce your best work when you aren't afraid to take risks, to endure criticism or embarrassment or even failure. Trusting your deepest intuitions and instincts may mean overriding contrary research, peer pressure, conventional wisdom, or intimidation."

I sometimes ask: Is a leader designated, are there followers, and is there a vision, goal or direction? But if people don't want to go, it doesn't matter if the goal is interesting. People naturally seek meaning. When Steve Jobs recruited John Scully to join Apple Computer, a start-up company then, Scully was the number two guy at Pepsi-Cola and heir apparent to the chairman of this multi-billion dollar company. Scully initially refused the job. Why leave Pepsi for a four-year-old company? But, he found it hard saying no to Steve Jobs. "He just stared at me and said, 'Do you want to sell sugar water for the rest of your life or do you want to come with me and change the world?' I decided to go, because I knew I would wonder for the rest of my life what I would have missed."

Whenever you miss working with a dynamic leader—one who is continuously learning new tricks—on a project with real meaning, you miss a lot.

TRICK #3

Lead from Voice
and Vision

What's so tricky about leading from voice and vision, rather than leading from position and perceived power? The underlying issue in leading from voice is trust; in fact, I believe that trust is the underlying issue in not only getting people on your side, but having them stay there. Leading from voice is a necessary condition for movement leadership, or for any situation—such as the Girl Scouts or the Red Cross—where the leader is dealing with volunteers, free agents, and free spirits (today's work force).

Frances Hesselbein, former chief executive of the Girl Scouts and current leader of the Drucker Foundation, notes: "The challenge for leaders is to build a cohesive community both within and outside the organization, to invest in relationships, and to communicate a vision that speaks to a richly diverse workforce and marketplace."

Clarify the vision. The critical factor for success in any venture is a shared vision among associates. If you're not sure of the vision of your company, how can you tell what the advantage of an alliance would be? You must be certain you have the right map and compass before embarking on the journey.

What people want most from their leaders is vision and direction, purpose and meaning, trust and truth. Leaders create a vision with meaning—one with significance, one that puts the players at the center of things rather than at the periphery.

A vision can be shared only if it has meaning for the people involved in it. You can't be the only one making decisions. You can't be the only leader. Rather you have to create an environment in which people at all levels are empowered to be leaders, to subscribe to your vision, and to make effective decisions.

To communicate a vision, you need more than words, speeches, memos, and laminated plaques. You need to live a vision, day in, day out—embodying it and empowering every other person to execute that vision in everything he or she does, anchoring it in realities so that it becomes a template for decision making. Actions do speak louder than words.

If you think your company's vision lacks definition, you may want to address some questions that may help give it color and dimension:

- What is unique about us?
- What values are true priorities for the next year?
- What would make me professionally commit my mind and heart to this vision over the next five to 10 years?
- What does the world need that our company can and should provide?
- What do I want our company to accomplish so that I will be committed, aligned, and proud of my association with it?

Ask yourself those questions today. Your answers will be the fire that heats the forge of your company's future.

Manage the dream. Leaders manage the dream. All leaders have the capacity to create a compelling vision, one that takes people to a new place, and the ability to translate that vision into reality.

Jung said: "A dream that is not understood remains a mere occurrence. Understood, it becomes a living experience."

Jim Burke, CEO of Johnson & Johnson, spends 40 percent of his time communicating the company's credo. More than 800 managers have attended J&J "challenge meetings," where they go through the credo line by line to see what changes need to be made. Over the years, some of those changes have been fundamental. But like the U.S. Constitution, the credo itself endures.

General Electric CEO Jack Welch said: "Yesterday's idea of the boss, who became the boss because he or she knew one more fact than the person working for them, is yesterday's manager.

Tomorrow's person leads through a set of shared values, a shared objective, a vision."

The single defining quality of leaders is the capacity to create and realize a vision. Yeats said, "In dreams begins responsibility." Vision is a waking dream.

The leader's responsibility is to transform the vision into reality. In doing so, they transform their dominion—whether an airline, a motion picture, or an entire industry.

Henry David Thoreau put it this way: "If one advances confidently in the direction of his dreams, and endeavors to live the life he has imagined, he will meet with a success in common hours. If you have built castles in the air, your work need not be lost. It is where they should be. Now put the foundation under them."

The times demand leaders who can manage the dream by creating a vision and then translating that vision into reality. In the course of my research, I've learned something about the current crop of leaders, and something about the kind of leadership that will be necessary to forge the future. While leaders come in every size, shape and disposition—short, tall, neat, sloppy, young, old, male, and female—every leader shares a common trait: a concern with a guiding purpose, a directing goal, an overarching vision.

Managing the dream has five parts: (1) communicating the vision; (2) recruiting meticulously; (3) rewarding; (4) retraining; and (5) reorganizing. All five parts of managing the dream are exemplified by Jan Carlzon, CEO of SAS. Carlzon's vision was to make SAS one of the five or six remaining international carriers. To accomplish this, he developed two goals: (1) to make SAS 1 percent better in a 100 different ways from its competitors; and (2) to create a market niche. Carlzon chose the business traveler, because he believed that this was the most profitable niche—rather than college students, or travel agent deals, or any of the other choices. To attract business travelers, Carlzon had to make their every interaction with every SAS employee rewarding. He had to endow with purpose and relevance, courtesy and caring, every single interaction—and he estimated that there were 63,000 of these interactions per day between SAS employees and current or potential customers. He called these interactions "moments of truth."

Carlzon developed a marvelous cartoon book, *The Little Red Book*, to communicate the new SAS vision to employees. And he set up a corporate college in Copenhagen to train them. He debureaucratized the whole organization. The organization chart no longer looked like a pyramid—it looked like a set of circles, a galaxy. In fact, Carlzon's book, which is called *Moments of Truth* in English, is titled *Destroying the Pyramids* in Swedish.

One circle or segment, is the Copenhagen-New York route. All the pilots, the navigators, the engineers, the flight attendants, the baggage handlers, the reservations agents—everybody who has to do with the Copenhagen-New York route—are involved in a self-managed, autonomous work group with a gain-sharing plan so that they all participate in whatever increment of profits that particular route brings in. There's also a Copenhagen-Frankfurt segment, and so on. The corporation is structured in terms of these small, egalitarian groups.

When you lead from voice and vision, your dreams are more likely to come true.

Leading with Wisdom. Leadership has become something of a national obsession. Books almost cascade from the shelves. A recent study looked at the reasons for removing CEOs, and found ineffective leadership to be fairly high at 73 percent. Another study, at the Harvard Business School, showed that a CEO is 10 times more likely to be removed for poor performance today than 20 years ago. If you look at the major icons of American industry over the past 10 years, almost all the top CEOs have been dumped. Another study found that companies that are perceived to be well led have a much higher growth rate. Clearly, if asked to pick the factor that makes the most difference, you'd pick leadership. As Jack Welch told me: "My job is simple. I have three things to do. I pick the right people, I allocate the right resources to my 15 business units, and I transmit ideas with the speed of light. Ideas are what count. All these interactions are just building the idea pyramid."

Some people naturally seem to have that capacity to create an environment where ideas are generated. Such capacity strikes at the core of who you are. I think that core changes over time, but character means something that's not superficial. You can't put a person into a microwave and out pops the McLeader. It doesn't happen like that. Leadership is something that evolves.

What do most people want from their leadership? I think they want: meaning and direction, trust, a sense of hope and optimism, and results. These are the bottom-line issues. Great leaders provide the culture to make authentic human relationships possible. They have a sense of hardiness—an expectation of a positive outcome and some bias toward action, risk, curiosity, courage, and results. Exemplary leaders are people with conviction, commitment, resolve and passion. Yes, leadership has to do with vision, discernment and insight, but it is also about knowing not just where you're going but where you've been and where you are now. The great world leaders have all had that helicopter view.

When we consider what goes into trust in work relationships with a boss, events surrounding President Bill Clinton are instructive. Even before publication of the Starr Report, most people thought Clinton was lying about his activity in the Oval Office, and yet they still thought he was doing a splendid job, largely based on their perception of the strength of the economy.

When I talk about trust in leadership, I imagine a tripod of interdependent forces that all leaders have to some extent. All leaders have a certain degree of ambition or drive along with competence (or business literacy) and integrity or moral discernment. Most of the exemplary leaders I know seem to have these three in balance. It's hard to imagine someone with integrity but who lacks the other two qualities; maybe Hamlet fits the bill as a person with good motives but no competence or drive.

One of the most important criteria of mental health is an accurate perception of reality, but it seems to me that many great leaders have an almost unwarranted optimism—a "can-do" mentality. They have this sense of possibility. Most optimists consider themselves to be lucky and have a positive outlook. President Reagan was the perfect example, although there were times when

I thought his optimism was unwarranted. Ultimately, after all the meetings and pronouncements, you've got to act—and that can be difficult. People who have brilliant ideas often need someone else to translate them into action. Leaders need managers. Without them, leaders are like lonely poets. Although strong management—too many meetings, too much bureaucracy, too much specialization—stifles innovation and intellectual capital, vision by itself means nothing. Contemplation and elegant illuminations don't mean a thing unless they are followed by action.

TRICK #4

Build and Sustain Trust

One key attribute of the new leader is the ability to generate and sustain trust. Largely as a result of downsizing, the level of trust in the workplace is at its lowest ebb ever. Terrible alienation exists in today's plants and offices, with corporate leaders tending to regard employees not as the company's treasure, but as a fiscal liability, and employees feeling the hopelessness of poet John Milton's Samson, "eyeless in Gaza, at the mill with slaves."

The only great work being done in many businesses today is that of entrepreneurial individuals who are using their employers' fax machines and other resources to craft their next job—a high-anxiety activity that has been dubbed "wing-walking." Only a leader who inspires trust can get such workers off the wing and focused on the tasks that the organization deems important. Such a leader sends the message that "We are all in this together."

But the same ability to inspire and persuade through empathy and trust can be and should be present in all organizations. In his book *Leadership Is an Art,* Max De Pree, CEO of Herman Miller, argues that's the best way to treat everyone.

Leading with trust. Trust is what makes organizations function or not function well. After downsizing and changes, there's a general mistrust. For example, I once received a letter from a CEO of a Fortune 100 company who said, "I know where we need to be in the near future, but we have thousands of employees who don't want to go there and won't let us position ourselves. They want the world to be the way it used to be, and they are not willing to accept any alternative forecast."

What's fascinating about this leader is that it's a trust factor. Behind his back, his direct reports refer to him as either Darth Vader or The Blade. This is a leader who has imagination and vision, but he doesn't have the trust of his people. He is smart, but he fails to build consensus. Without trust, you will find it hard to lead, especially when many people are concerned about their jobs.

Trust is one of those fragile things that is hard to create and so easy to lose. We still see many managers and leaders running companies by short-term numbers, even though it's apparent that short-termism will not work in the long run. GE's Jack Welch says that if you're a high school basketball coach, you can shout and shake the kids up, but you can't do that for 15 or 20 years in the same organization. "You may get away with it in the short run, but it won't work long term."

Five Prerequisites

What goes into a trusting relationship in business, marriage, friendship, or family? What makes you trust a boss, colleague, friend, or spouse? Leaders have five qualities that generate trust.

1. Competence. As a platoon leader in World War II, I know my platoon had to feel that they could trust my competence. Hollywood director Sydney Pollack can get the best actors to work with him because they know they will learn some things, and likely be nominated for an Academy Award, because he's got the competence. People want someone they can rely on, who's accountable. What I hear most about ineffective leaders is that they do whatever the last person they spoke to recommended. If you work for someone like that, you're in for many surprises. I like to ask CEOs, "Around here, what's the mean time between surprises?"

Real leaders are people of strong character who generate and sustain trust. To trust their leaders and to have confidence in them, people need to see evidence of competence. They have to see their leaders as worthy of their trust by virtue of their character and competence.

2. Constancy. In a changing world, you have to be agile, adept, athletic, adaptive—but, your principles have to be constant. You need a reliable set of standards of behavior. One of my weaknesses as a university president was that I would get excited by some new idea, and I would come into the staff meeting with my top people, and say, "Why don't we do this?" I wasn't as constant, in retrospect, as I would have liked to have been. In fact, one of my vice-presidents told me that my nickname was Warren *Vision de jour* Bennis. Constancy suggests that whatever surprises leaders themselves may face, they don't create any surprises for the group. Leaders are all of a piece; they stay the course. They are reliable. Leaders are there when it counts—they are ready to support their coworkers in the moments that matter.

One thing you hear about the least effective leaders is that they do whatever the last person they spoke to recommended or that they plunge forward with the latest good idea that pops into their heads. Before followers can trust a leader, they have to know what to expect. So sometimes leaders have to put off their grand ideas or glorious opportunities until they have had a chance to convince their allies of the value of their ideas. In business, as in politics, the effectiveness of a decision is the quality of the decision multiplied by the acceptance of it.

3. Caring. Caring is compassion, empathy, the capacity to understand what other people are feeling. Caring is lacking in many leaders because they fail to practice empathy, to practice putting themselves in another person's shoes. I've seen more executives fail for this lack than any other when it comes to interpersonal skills: the lack of being able to understand. Effective leaders show that they care by how they communicate. Most communication has to be done eyeball to eyeball rather than in newsletters, on videos, or via satellite. One of the best ways to build trust and show caring is by deep listening. When people feel that they are being heard and understood, you achieve the most powerful dynamic of human interaction. Listening doesn't mean agreeing, but it does mean having the empathic reach to understand another. I think if people feel that you care, they are more resilient to bad news. They can bounce back, simply because they still care about the company and its people and products.

4. Candor. The lack of candor is one of the biggest tragedies in organizations because we don't speak truth to power. And so people who know the truth don't speak the truth where it would help. In my own study, I discovered that seven out of ten people will not speak up even if they know that what their boss is going to do is going to get him and the company in trouble. They will not be candid. They are not encouraged to speak up—they see dissenters being punished, not rewarded, and so the truth never gets out. There is no incentive for speaking up.

Leaders must be candid in their communications. I can't overemphasize the importance of encouraging openness, even dissent. I recognize that there is also a danger in presenting a strong point of view: it can intimidate others and shut down communication. And such kinks in the communication lines can prove deadly. So, what's a leader to do? A leader needs candor to operate effectively. Unfortunately, most people in organizations don't speak up if they think their point of view will vary from the conventional wisdom or their boss's point of view. A leader needs to cultivate firm-minded subordinates with the wisdom and courage to say no. That means the leader needs to be trusted as a fair and honest person of integrity, someone who does not kill the messenger who tells the truth. When you have to make a tough decision, I think what you can do, what a company can do, what any leader can do, is be candid, communicative, and caring. If people feel they've been given a fair deal, if they understand the reasons for the actions, they will be in better shape. Rather than sabotage the move, they will likely support it.

5. Character. What all these behaviors and skills surrounding trust add up to is integrity, and that means character. A leader with drive but not competence and integrity is a demagogue. One with competence but not integrity and drive is a technocrat. One with ambition and competence but not integrity is a destructive achiever. Leaders have to earn respect to generate and sustain trust. Only leaders who inspire trust based on character can keep people focused on the important tasks. Character isn't a superficial style. The word comes from an ancient Greek verb meaning "to engrave" and its related noun means "mark" or "distinctive quality." In French it means "inscribed." It's not dressing for success—it's who we are as persons. Leaders have integrity and congruity—they honor their commitments and promises. They walk their talk. In true leaders, there is no gap between the theories they espouse and the lives they practice.

I have always believed that leadership is, above all, a question of character. Ironically, character is always the last criterion used to evaluate corporate leaders, who are usually judged on relatively easy to assess but far less important criteria.

Successful leadership is not about being tough or soft, assertive or sensitive. It is about having a particular set of attributes—ones all leaders, male and female, seem to share. And chief among these attributes is character.

E. B. White once said, "I wake up every morning determined both to change the world and have one hell of a good time. Sometimes this makes planning the day a little difficult." Every leader today shares a similar wake-up call and charge—both to change the world and to have a good time doing it. But the noble mission of a leader can't be used to justify the means. In the leadership arena, character counts. I am not saying this casually. My convictions about character-based leadership come from years of studies, observations, and interviews with leaders and with the people near them. Leaders have vision and a strongly defined sense of purpose, they inspire trust, and they work for change. Thus one way to define leadership is a character in action.

Most organizations evaluate their executives and managers using these seven criteria: technical competence or business literacy (knowledge of the territory), people skills (capacity to motivate people), conceptual skills (ability to put things together), results (track record), taste (capacity to choose terrific people most of the time), judgment (ability to make wise decisions in a fog of reality and uncertainty), and character (integrity to walk the talk). The stakes are high for both individuals and organizations. So it's worth knowing more about the character component of successful leadership.

I also believe, however, that our character is continuously evolving. I don't think character is fixed at age six.

If we keep learning, our character evolves. I know that I'm evolving. My character is changing as a result of my experiences. For example, I recently came upon my first passport (1951), and I looked at my signature. I saw my signature as a metaphor for character, because although my signature then is like my signature today, it also is different. It has evolved. Nuances developed. It's shaped differently now, although you can still see the basic DNA of it, it's different than it was in 1951.

Becoming a leader is much the same as becoming an integrated human being. In his biography of President Truman, David McCullough wrote: "Character counts in the presidency more than any other single quality. When the chips are down, how do you decide an issue? Which way do you go? What courage is called on?" Now, I have never seen anybody derailed, plateaued, fired, or passed over because of a lack of technical competence. But, I've seen many people get derailed because of poor judgment and character. These are the hardest things to teach because it's so difficult to get at judgment and character.

If you hope to build and sustain trust, care about character.

TRICK #5

Maintain Credibility

When you downsize an organization, reengineer the work, and restructure the relationships, you alter the culture dramatically: the vision often changes; the values of the leaders are altered; and trust begins to wane. Everyone starts asking, "What's going on here?" And they start getting very worried about their jobs and future prospects with the firm.

This is common in small and large firms everywhere. For example, when I spoke on leadership at a Fortune 100 firm, I emphasized some traditional aspects of leadership, such as a sense of purpose, the capacity to generate trust, and a bias toward action and risk taking. Most people in the audience were in their early 40s. They listened to me very responsively, taking notes and paying careful attention. However, they acknowledged a very disheartening disconnect between my "marvelous ideas" and their own reality. It went beyond questioning whether my ideas were well-founded. They were saying that because of downsizing and restructuring, they never know from one day to the next whether they still have a job. So, how do you maintain trust to lead in an environment where no one's job is secure?

Efforts to improve competitiveness by cutting costs and becoming leaner result in major leadership challenges. When trust declines, people's commitment to their current organization declines. So, how do you create an empowered organization during radical reengineering and layoffs? This problem will be with us for at least another decade.

In the past, downturns lasted only two or three years. If you were laid off, you could count on being hired by someone else or hired back by the very firm that let you go. However, today this rarely happens. Organizations are not trimming down to meet temporary economic downturns. They are trimming down for the long run. When they let someone go, there is no plan to rehire the person. The old idea that those who were thrown out of work because of competitive pressures would soon find positions in new, innovative firms that could survive no longer holds.

Companies can generate more output and profit with fewer people. In fact, Charles Handy wrote about a CEO who boasted that his equation for success was "half times two times three equals success." The CEO was saying that, with half the work force, he could produce twice as many goods and generate three times as much profit. These are impressive numbers, but they fail to answer the question: What happens to the other 50 percent of the work force that gets laid off? And since no one knows for sure whether they'll make the cut, trust and commitment decline. People are concerned about their own fate, and the organization suffers as a result.

The lack of trust is likely to impede performance because the company's intellectual capital is being diminished. The best ideas, innovations, inventions, and reinventions are less than they would be under ideal conditions. Rather than feel empowered, people feel disempowered, frightened, anxious, and scared. This will be the major challenge for leaders in the 21st century.

How does a leader create a sense of trust and maintain credibility in a downsized organization if employees are constantly worrying about getting pink slips?

The way downsizing is typically done in most Fortune 100 firms is to reduce the size of the workforce dramatically. In its first phase of downsizing, General Electric went from 425,000 to 275,000 in about three years. But amazingly, CEO Jack Welch and his team managed to generate even more employee empowerment and sustain trust and credibility during this time of massive layoffs in 14 divisions within the company. So, this Draconian approach to downsizing can work, even though the fallout on survivors is often serious.

FOUR WAYS TO KEEP UP IN A DOWNTURN

Assume, for example, you are in the midst of downsizing and trying to generate and sustain trust. There are a number of ways—none of them fully satisfactory, but all of them are better than what happened at the gross example of Al Dunlap at Scott Paper and Bob Allen at AT&T, which are egregious and obscene examples of how downsizing shouldn't be done.

Of course, what happened at Scott Paper with Al Dunlap, the man who takes pride in being called "Chainsaw Al," was most obscene, particularly because of his predominant idea that the only thing that really matters in an organization is maximizing profit for the shareholders.

When I first began reading Dunlap's book *Mean Business,* I thought of former Chief Justice Oliver Wendell Holmes' statement: "I wouldn't give a fig for the simplicity this side of complexity, but I would give my right arm for the simplicity on the other side of complexity." Because what's wrong with Dunlap and other leaders like him is that they see the world through narrow, skewed lenses. Mean business is exactly what it is. And in a mean environment, you can't generate trust. I can't imagine that the workforce was particularly productive or empowered when mean Chainsaw Al was operating.

1. One way is to emphasize employability. Many large organizations are saying that they can't guarantee lifetime employment. But they do help educate their employees so that they can get jobs elsewhere. They say, "We're going to educate and train you because we care about your employability. If we find it necessary to lay you off, we want to help you get a job somewhere else."

2. Another response is that of an Emersonian self-reliance. You might tell people, "Look, you cannot depend on this or any other organization for lifetime security. You've got to educate yourself. You've got to be self-reliant." Don't think that large organizations are any more secure than small ones. My guess is that very few of the big monsters will survive in the long run. So, forget the whole ethos of the organization man or woman. Many companies encourage employees to take night courses, to get an Executive MBA, but not to depend on them.

3. Allow, even encourage, dissent—and reward good ideas.
When downsizing is appropriate, as it sometimes is, and necessary, as it often is, leaders must be open and candid. For those who leave, the candor will be healing. And for those who stay, open communication will make the company a psychologically safe place to work.

I'd always rather err on the side of openness. But there's a difference between optimum and maximum openness, and fixing that boundary is a judgment call. The art of leadership is knowing how much information to pass on to keep people motivated and to be as honest and up front as you can be. But, there are real limits to what you can share.

Why do so many companies and teams fail? Do the troops lose faith in the leader? Is the chemistry all wrong? Certainly, there is a loss of confidence in the leader and the leader's ability to be coached back to the right track. Real dissent is rarely addressed openly. The leaders don't want to hear dissent, and soon the dissenters are no longer invited to the meetings. So, you're hearing only one voice. You circle the wagons. You stop listening to as many sources as you can. You get dissent which is public and not internal, because you domesticate it.

Great leaders encourage dissent. Their organizations are verbal, argumentative entities. They play Frisbee with ideas. The culture is noisy. People feel free to express themselves. In such organizations, there is always this give and take, the freedom to explore different (crazy) ideas without being cut down, and an incredible amount of rejoicing and celebrating. There is also a sense that good ideas pay off. Groups that fail are just the opposite. They cover up. They don't encourage different ideas; they don't reward them. Failure is not tolerated. When you work with a real leader, you know that you're in the hands of a very competent person. And that makes you and the rest of the group do more than you thought you could.

4. Involve people in change. In recent years, such concepts as involvement, participation, and empowerment have progressed from being esoteric ideas to being widely taken for granted. However, dramatic changes in the environment are having a significant impact. I see the notion of empowerment on a collision course with many ideas associated with downsizing, restructuring, and reengineering. But real leaders can steer clear of collisions. Indeed, as Charles Dickens intimated, even the worst of times can be the best of times.

Realistically, in the short run I can't see any scenarios in which restructuring and downsizing can coexist with involvement and empowerment. In the long run, I think, yes, there are cases where it has worked. Again, think about the General Electric example, where they downsized gradually over a period of three years. When it was over, the company could say, "That's it. We've cut all we want to cut," I think at that time you can start rebuilding credibility.

TRICK #6

Imbue Work with Meaning

Great leaders imbue even the most mundane work with meaning and turn even tedious activities into inspirational missions that people rally around. We can do so much better than we do by reminding people of the meaning of their work.

The late Richard Feynman, the irrepressible Nobel Prize-winning physicist, used to tell a wonderful story that illustrates how profoundly meaning can transform work. Among Feynman's tasks during the Manhattan Project was supervising a group of technicians who had been brought to Los Alamos, New Mexico, from all over the country to do calculations on primitive computers.

The work involved doing energy calculations and other tasks crucial to the success of the project, but, unlike Feynman and the other physicists, the technicians were kept in the dark about the true nature of the project or even what their calculations meant. They did what they were ordered to do: process one number after another, but they did it slowly and badly. And then Feynman prevailed on his superiors to lift the veil of secrecy. J. Robert Oppenheimer talked to the technicians, explaining how important it was to build the bomb before the enemy did and their vital role in that effort.

As a result, the men were transformed. They found new, better ways of doing the work. They invented new programs. They worked through the night. Ever precise, Feynman determined that the group worked nearly 10 times faster after the task had been imbued with meaning.

Great leaders can bring about that kind of transformation. They have a vision, and they have the ability to articulate that vision in a way that makes other people want to sign up, too. Oppenheimer had that talent, but so do the best corporate leaders today. Sears, Roebuck & Co. CEO Arthur Martinez has transformed that once-failing retail giant by persuading employees that they are a crucial part, not of a mundane comeback effort, but of one of the greatest adventures in business history. CEO Herb Kelleher has made Southwest Airlines wildly successful by enlisting employees on a crusade: not to sell bargain airline tickets, but to give everyone a precious gift—the freedom of travel.

Exemplary leaders, like Herb Kelleher, bring out the best in their people by providing a meaningful workplace. People not only search for meaning in life, they also search for meaning in work. Is there such a thing as a meaningful workplace? If so, how does it look and feel? And what can leaders do to create it? Many people are still unfulfilled. The workplace keeps them busy, but their hearts and minds remain disengaged. There's a big difference between "job satisfaction" and "workplace meaning." For most people, "satisfaction" looks and feels like conformance to standards. Needs and expectations may be met, but meaning goes much deeper. In a meaningful workplace, it's less about needs and expectations and more about mission and possibilities and fulfillment.

People find "meaning" at work in different ways and from various sources. Each person has a unique set of priorities, but purpose is the common denominator. All people desire to make a difference. To strengthen the sense of meaning, effective leaders often talk about the purpose of the team, function, or organization. They know that people want to be full partners in the enterprise— in the sense of shaping what they do and how they do it. They also want the workplace to be more like a community where dialogue thrives, relationships unfold, and unity of purpose carries the day. People want a home for their talents and an open field to pursue their deep interests. Incentives or high pay alone can't build a meaningful workplace. Extrinsic motivators often aren't even mentioned when people talk about on-the-job fulfillment.

Every great group believes it is on a mission. Each is filled with gifted people who want to be working on their particular project more than anything else. Each is made up of people who didn't know the meaning of the word impossible. Each believes it is involved in a struggle against a Goliath-like enemy and becomes a world unto itself, with its own language, jokes and rituals. And perhaps most telling, each is filled with people having fun.

Great groups have leaders who devote themselves to unleashing the genius of their colleagues. Each constitutes a team in which each member, including the leader, is needed to create the collective magic and meaning. Too many workers today regard themselves as wage slaves, and too many workplaces are populated by individuals who see themselves as underutilized and undervalued. We can change that and turn every group into a great one if we imbue work with meaning.

Too few corporate leaders understand the craving to be part of something larger, and even fewer understand how to tap into that longing to turn individual workers into cohesive, productive groups.

Knowing that people would rather be on a crusade than simply at work is one of the gifts of the leader who creates a Great Group. The ability to enlist others is not some simple rhetorical trick. If it were, the bland mission statements cranked out by most corporations would actually inspire workers, instead of infuriating them, as they typically do. The ability to inspire reflects a profound understanding of human nature. People want to do good work. They want the hours they spend in the workplace to mean something more than the sum of the objects they produce.

When I think about leaders such as Bob Taylor at Palo Alto Research Center, I'm reminded of the story about Queen Victoria's two great prime ministers, William Gladstone and Benjamin Disraeli. Someone once observed that when you had dinner with Gladstone, you came away thinking he was the wittiest, most intelligent, most charming person you had ever met. When you dined with Disraeli, you were sure you were the wittiest, most intelligent, most charming person ever. Leaders in the tradition of Disraeli, Oppenheimer, and Taylor allow their groups to become great, and they also find their own greatness in the group.

Such leaders have contagious optimism. They make people feel that they can accomplish anything. They also understand the truth of playwright Noel Coward's observation that "work can be more fun than fun." The workplaces they create are productive because they are filled with people who are enjoying the intrinsic rewards of working well. We love to problem solve. It's the task we evolved for. We especially love to do it in partnership with others whom we respect.

The best people working for organizations are like volunteers. Since they could probably find good jobs in any number of groups, they choose to work somewhere for reasons less tangible than salary or position. They work because they find meaning in it.

Volunteers do not need contracts, they need covenants. Covenantal relationships induce freedom, not paralysis. A conventional relationship rests on shared commitment to ideas, to issues, to values, to goals, and to management process. Words such as love, warmth, and personal chemistry are certainly pertinent. Convenantal relationships fill deep needs and they enable work to have meaning and to be fulfilling.

TRICK #7

Create a Sense
of Community

The longing for community is born in all of us. Too few corporate leaders understand the depth of our craving to be part of something larger, and even fewer understand how to tap that longing to turn individual workers into a cohesive, productive group. And yet it is only in such groups that the increasingly complex work of the modern corporation can be accomplished.

Allowed to flourish, people spark greatness in each other. As Italian author Luciano De Crescenzo said so beautifully, "We are all angels with only one wing. We can only fly while embracing each other."

The best leaders today are creative leaders who build communities. Incredible change in technology and globalization has created great confusion. "If you're not confused," said one executive, "you don't know what's going on." You can't know what's going on if you only look at numbers. You need to hone your anticipation skills and exercise your creative imagination. But the size of corporations limits creativity. We're seeing the bureaucratization of imagination. We're witnessing shareholder-versus-stakeholder debates. Are corporations responsible to shareholders or to the community, the workers, and suppliers? How do you balance the needs of all stakeholders? Ultimately, you have to create a sense of community.

Trust keeps communities together. When workers see vision and mission statements framed in beautiful Lucite plaques on their walls, they want to see congruence between the talk and the walk. For example, most vision and value statements talk about how companies support multicultural diversity in the work force, yet many organizations are still incredibly biased toward minorities and women. We also note a growing disparity between the haves and have-nots. The average CEO salary is about 200 times more than the average work force salary. So, when you see this glaring discrepancy between what's going on in the workplace and what you see in vision statements, you tend to distrust your leaders. Disparities breed distrust, and distrust destroys community.

How can executives become more enlightened? I would suggest that executives read more. Many CEOs have no idea of the historical context of what they do. I recommend reading histories, biographies, and commentaries to avoid the trap of the command-and-control macho style of management.

You can't enjoy freedom and creativity within a corporate culture filled with dress codes, set hours and arbitrary regulations. Corporations must become theaters of inquiry that release brainpower. They need to generate intellectual capital ideas, innovation, and imagination. If rules, not values, determine behavior, you will see little success in creating a sense of community.

If we're going to get the best out of people, we have to give them a lot more autonomy and a sense of being self-managed. This causes a collective shiver down the backs of many executives, but that's because they don't understand motivation. When your people are more motivated and empowered, you actually gain influence.

Ultimately, a leader's ability to galvanize coworkers resides both in an understanding of self and in an understanding of coworkers' needs and wants, along with an understanding of what might be called their mission.

In such leaders, competence, vision, and virtue exist in nearly perfect balance. Competence, or knowledge, without vision and virtue, breeds technocrats. Virtue, without vision and knowledge, breeds ideologues. Vision, without virtue and knowledge, breeds demagogues.

As Peter Drucker has pointed out, the chief object of leadership is the creation of a human community held together by the work bond for a common purpose. Organizations and their leaders inevitably deal with the nature of man, which is why values, commitments, convictions, even passions are basic elements in any organization. Since leaders deal with people, not things, leadership without values, commitment, and conviction can only be inhumane and harmful.

Especially today, in the current volatile climate, it is vital that leaders steer a clear and consistent course. They must acknowledge uncertainties and deal effectively with the present, while simultaneously anticipating and responding to the future. This means endlessly expressing, explaining, extending, expanding, and, when necessary, revising the organization's mission. The goals are not ends, but ideal processes by which the future can be created.

Technology can aid communication and community building. There are discussion groups on the Internet, and you can stay in contact with people all over the world easily with e-mail.

But I don't think you can create a human community entirely by e-mail. There is a marvelous book called *The Well*, about one of the first Internet discussion groups in Marin County, California. But it wouldn't have been possible without a lot of human, face-to-face contact. It wasn't just being on e-mail together. There were self-help groups and chat rooms, but more than anything else, they picnicked together, they got to know each other, they went to each other for help. It wasn't simply an e-mail thing.

I do think that groups, intimacy, and collaboration can be augmented and accelerated with e-mail. I worked once with a group from Xerox—potential executives from various countries. They had been in e-mail contact for about 18 months, but this was their first meeting. Having been on e-mail that long, they connected more quickly. But I think you have to keep renewing that connection. And you can't do it solely by e-mail or distance learning.

At the University of Southern California, I teach an undergraduate class of 60 students, and we're all wired. That e-mail contact is very easy to do, but we also need small-group discussions. We get together four hours per week as a total group, and then we're also meeting in various subgroups throughout the week. You've got to have that human contact to create and sustain a sense of community.

TRICK #8

Become a Tomorrow Leader

The more authentic we become and the more attuned to the times, the better we can lead the transformation of our organizations.

Authentic people have a bias toward action. They keep saying, "You're never going to get anywhere if you keep sitting in the dugout." The only way you succeed, ultimately, in whatever you do is to get up there and take your swings—and sometimes that means taking a swing at someone else who you think is doing something wrong or dangerous for the company. That's action, too.

Every good leader has had a willful determination to achieve a set of goals, a set of convictions, about what he or she wanted the organization to achieve. In the leader, character is having the vision to see things not just the way they are but the way the should be—and doing something to make them that way. Leaders have the capacity to convert purpose and vision into action. It just isn't enough to have the great vision people can trust. It has to be manifest in some external products and results. Most leaders are pragmatic dreamers or practical idealists.

Most of the leaders that I've interviewed said they learn more from failure than from success. They possess the ability to learn from themselves and their mistakes, and know how to get the best and worst out of people. There is nothing like power to reveal your own humanity and character—especially power in crisis situations, because that's when you hit rock bottom. As one CEO told me, "That's when the iron enters your soul, and gives you resiliency to cope." There's nothing like being a person of responsibility that teaches you about who you are. Nothing.

Many companies are the direct reflection of their leaders. Effective leaders are all about creative collaboration, about creating a shared sense of purpose. A central task for the leader is the development of other leaders, creating conditions that enhance the ability of all employees to make decisions and create change. The leader actively helps his or her followers to reach their full potential. As Max De Pree once put it: "The signs of outstanding leadership appear primarily among the followers."

How do you go about becoming a good leader? Figure out what you're good at. Hire only good people who care and treat them the way you want to be treated. Identify your one or two key objectives or directions and ask your coworkers how to get there. Listen hard and get out of their way. Cheer them. Switch from macho to maestro.

TEN TRAITS

Tomorrow's leaders must learn how to create an environment that embraces change, not as a threat but as an opportunity. Some leaders will be successful at this; others will fail.

1. Successful leaders have self-awareness and self-esteem. They sense when a different repertoire of competencies are needed, without being threatened by the need to change. They have the diagnostic ability to understand what new things are required, or what things should be unlearned, plus the behavioral flexibility to change. GE's Jack Welch had enough diagnostic ability to say, "The way I was doing things is not going to work," and then he was also able to change his behavior.

2. Leaders ensure that boundaries are porous and permeable. You need the foresight to see things before the curve, before others do. And the only way you get that is by being in touch with your customers, with society, with the outside world, by having the boundaries permeable and porous enough to get your information. That's why people at the periphery are usually the most creative and often the least consulted.

3. Competitive advantage will be the leadership of women. I suspect that, by the year 2005, about 50 percent of the vice presidents for finance will be women and women will appear much more often in top management positions. One of our competitive advantages will be the full deployment of the talent of women in our workforce. We must dispel the myths that the only way for a woman to succeed is to act like a man. One irony is that male leaders have been trying to shed the same macho character traits that women have been encouraged to imitate. Dr. Helen Tartakoff, a Harvard psychoanalyst, said that, generally, women have exactly the opposite character traits, and that these feminine traits contain the potential for improving the human condition.

What has got to change is not women's character traits but corporate cultures, because most of them have been playing male-chauvinist games for too long. The power structures and avenues of opportunity have excluded women for years.

Successful leadership doesn't depend on masculinity or femininity. It's not about being tough or soft, assertive or sensitive. It's about having a particular set of attributes which all leaders, both male and female, seem to share.

4. Leaders have a strongly defined sense of purpose and vision. They also develop the capacity to articulate it clearly. Leading means doing the right things, while managing just means doing things right. Too many organizations are overmanaged and underled because the people at the top are better at making policies, practices and procedures than they are at creating a compelling, overarching vision. They are managers, not leaders. They are looking at how to achieve greater efficiency and how to control their systems and structures more effectively. They are looking at how to do things right.

We need more leaders, people who do the right things. Managers are people who do things right. There's a profound difference. When you think about doing the right things, your mind immediately goes toward thinking about the future, thinking about dreams, missions, visions, strategic intents, and purposes. When you think about doing things right, you think about systems and processes. You think about how-to. Leaders ask the what and why questions, not the how questions. Leaders think about empowerment, not control. And empowerment means not stealing responsibility from people. Grace Hopper, a management expert who was the first woman admiral in the U.S. Navy, has said, "You manage things, but you lead people."

Tomorrow's leaders will spend much of their time nurturing and developing other leaders within the organization. Today's leaders need to prepare themselves and their people for the challenges of tomorrow. Over the years, I studied many terrific groups, many creative collaborators. And in every case where they really reached epiphanies, there was a leader who enrolled people in an exciting, insanely significant vision. Someone who was capable of reeling in advocates and supporters to work with him or her. They all believed that they would make a dent in the universe. What leaders need to realize is that people would much rather live a life dedicated to an idea or a cause that they believe in, than lead a life of aimless diversion. Effective leaders are all about cause and meaning—creating a shared sense of purpose. Because people need purpose. That's why we live. And the power of an organization will be that shared sense of purpose. With a shared sense of purpose, you can achieve anything.

In the twenty-first century, we will need leaders who know what is important in the long term. Who have a vision, dream, mission, or a strategic intent. Who remind people continually of what's important and create an environment where people know why they are there.

To communicate a vision, you need more than words, speeches, memos, and laminated plaques. You need to live a vision, day in, day out, embodying it and empowering every other person to execute that vision in everything he or she does, anchoring it in realities, so that it becomes a template for decision making. Actions do speak louder than words.

5. Leaders generate trust. Leaders will have to be candid in their communications and show that they care. They've got to be seen to be trustworthy. Most communication has to be done eyeball-to-eyeball, rather than in newsletters, on videos, or via satellite. The leader must generate and sustain trust, and that also means demonstrating competence and constancy.

"Strike hard and try everything," wrote Henry James. You're never going to get anywhere unless you risk and try, and then learn from each experience. Leaders have to play even when it means making mistakes. And they have to learn from those mistakes.

6. Leaders have a bias toward action. Not just reflection, but action. A combination of both of them, of course, is what we all want. And then you need to get feedback on how you are doing. You have to cultivate sources of reflective backtalk by getting people around you whose counsel you treasure, people who are capable of telling the truth, people you can depend on, people who have the future in their bones. You need these people. You can't do it alone. You need people who can take the vision and run with it.

7. Leaders create not just a vision, but a vision with meaning—one with significance, one which puts the players at the center of things rather than at the periphery. If companies have a vision that is meaningful to people, nothing will stop them from being successful. Not just any old vision will do; it must be a shared vision with meaning and significance.

The only way a vision can be shared is for it to have meaning for the people who are involved in it. Leaders have to specify the steps that behaviorally fit into that vision, and then reward people for following those steps. Then they need some feedback loops, to make sure that the vision is still relevant, salient, and has some resonance. Again, without meaning and resonance, vision statements are only stale truths.

8. Leaders must become very comfortable with advanced technology and the changes that it will bring. On my 70th birthday, my children were all there; they're in their late 20s and early 30s. And one of their birthday gifts to me was two hours of instruction on using the Internet and the World Wide Web. Two of them gave me gifts of software.

In this high-tech, high-touch world, we're going to see a totally new breed of people for whom advanced technology is just a natural part of life. Leaders will have to be not only comfortable with advanced technology but at the same time engage even more hands-on than ever before. They will also need more interpersonal competence.

9. Leaders must act big if they are small, and small if they are big. What we see in the global economy is that both small and big companies can be successful. It's just a matter of finding the right scale for a particular organization and industry, and then providing the right structure and leadership.

As Rosabeth Moss Kanter points out, companies worldwide are becoming PALs: they are "pooling, allying, and linking." This is particularly true of small companies, who are creating networks, joint ventures, R&D consortia, and strategic partnerships that cut across corporate and national boundaries. They are "buying the power of bigness," as Jay Galbraith says, to gain scale in marketing, purchasing, and manufacturing.

Small firms also have new technologies on their side. Like computer-based manufacturing and distribution, sophisticated marketing databases, the latest telecommunication systems—all of which are formidable competitive weapons that allow them to build global markets quickly.

But this in no way signals the end of the large corporation. Giant companies have some very formidable advantages— economies of scale, resources, skilled people, know-how, social clout, long-term planning, and stability. They just wish they could get all the benefits of size without all the problems of bureaucracy and the other diseconomics of scale that size brings with it. To compete, these giants have got to behave like small, fast-moving companies. They have to recreate themselves as collections of small, independent, manageable units. Hence the worldwide focus on reengineering, downsizing, subcontracting, decentralization, spin-offs, and intrapreneuring.

10. Ultimately, leaders make federations of corporations. Most successful organizations combine the best characteristics of both big and small companies. The most practical solution, particularly for the large corporation, is federalism. Federations work better than monolithic organizations because, along with strength, they offer flexibility. They are more nimble and adaptive. They have all the inherent advantages of being big but all the benefits of being small.

Everywhere we look in the world today, from A&B to Benetton and from General Electric to Coca-Cola, we see new corporate confederations made up of numerous semi-autonomous units, all collaborating together and joined by a common vision.

Essentially, what makes a federation work are the principles described by James Madison in the late 18th century They are just as valid for corporations as they are for nations. First, you diffuse power to all the semi-autonomous units to become non-centralized, not just decentralized. Second, decision making must be shared between the units and the central authority. Nobody dictates terms and conditions to anybody else. Everything is negotiated. Third, there is an overarching vision and purpose, and some form of written constitution that lays out the company's operating principles. The units may even have their own constitutions, but they must be in harmony with the vision and principles of the federation. Fourth, the units need to understand where their boundaries are, whether these are business or product line boundaries or, as is the case with Coca-Cola's bottlers and Benetton's retailers, geographic boundaries. Fifth, you need to balance power not only between the units and the central authority, but between the units themselves, so that none of the units dominates the others. Sixth, the units must have autonomy. They have to be free to be self-governing, as long as they don't violate the federation's universal operating principles. And this is the most difficult characteristic of federalism. It's the source of the continuing tension: the power of the central authority versus the power of constituent units.

In many cases, this tension can be fatal, because the tendency is to go to one of the extremes. Either the federation overgeneralizes, or it lacks a unifying vision and constitution to hold it all together, and it finally disintegrates. So this is where you need true leadership. Leaders provide the necessary balance. Leaders of federations don't think of their associates as troops. And associates don't think of their leaders as generals. The leader of the new federal corporation has to be a leader of leaders. You can't be the only one making decisions. Rather, you have to create an environment in which other leaders, who subscribe to your vision, can make effective decisions—an environment in which people at all levels are empowered to be leaders.

One of my favorite metaphors for this is Schumacher's balloon man—now perhaps a woman—who holds a fistful of strings attached to balloons, each representing an entrepreneurial unit. She doesn't control the balloons—they all have their own individual buoyancy—but instead, she simply holds them together in her hand.

The leader of federations must have faith in the power of people to solve their problems locally. He or she is responsible for establishing the why and the what—the overarching vision and purpose—but the rest of the leaders are responsible for the how.

Coca-Cola is a global federation of fiercely independent franchised bottlers and distributors. The late CEO Roberto Goizueta once had a meeting with these folks and asked them three times in one speech to please paint your trucks red. He didn't command them to do it. He pleaded with them.

Percy Barnevik, CEO of Asea Brown Boveri, describes his organization as "a federation of national companies with a global communications center." ABB has only 100 employees in its Zurich headquarters, but I've heard Barnevik say he has 5,000 leaders. So its not the central staff that holds ABB together, it's the common vision of globalism and excellence that those 5,000 leaders subscribe to. And, again, this is what I mean by a leader of leaders. Percy Barnevik doesn't command and control the troops. He simply enunciates clearly the company's performance standards and then he gives his associates the freedom to find the best ways of achieving those standards. He doesn't try to manage their jobs for them.

Tricks and Team Treats

Ghosts are haunting the halls of many organizations, making Halloween an everyday holiday. But if you hope to receive treats, you need to learn the trick of ghostbusting.

Many of us "old dogs" grew up in organizations dominated by the thoughts and actions of the Fords, Taylors, and Webers—the fathers of the classic bureaucratic system. Bureaucracy was a splendid social invention in its time, the 19th century. In his deadly prose, German sociologist, Max Weber, first brought to the world's attention that the machine model was ideal for harnessing the manpower and resources of the Industrial Revolution. To this day, many organizations and individual leaders retain the macho, control-and-command mentality that is intrinsic to that increasingly threadbare mode.

However much CEOs differ in experience and personal style, they constitute a prism through which the fortunes of the modern world are refracted. These leaders are emblematic of their time, forced to deal not only with the exigencies of their own organizations but also with a new social reality. Among the broader factors that underlie all their decisions: the accelerating rate and complexity of change, the emergence of new technologies, dramatic demographic shifts, and globalization.

Once I spoke with Alvin Toffler, the all-time change maven and author of the paradigm-shifting book, *Future Shock*. We were trying to name one organization that exists in today's environment that is immune to change and has been stable and prosperous. We couldn't think of one.

So, don't kid yourself. You are not immune. I suggest that you learn the tricks in this section—and thereby win the treats.

Increase Revenue and Share the Wealth

Sometimes I wonder if it ever occurs to leaders that there is another option to downsizing when cash become tight. This option smacks of the obvious, but then this would not be the first time I have accused leaders of overlooking the obvious: to increase revenues.

Increase revenue. Downsizing should be a last, not the first, resort to the problem of financial losses. The first response should be to increase revenues. I think that's the only way leaders are going to maintain trust over the long run. When we get to the place in our society where workers are feeling more secure about their skills and where their skills are as transportable as their health insurance, I think we will achieve a much higher quality of life.

Why not take the changes created by technology and increased productivity and invite people into an imaginary planet where they are free to release their brainpower and think of ways not just to cut costs, but to increase revenues. The first thing that management does in tough situations is to reduce the workforce, and reengineer or redesign to cut costs. But you can't reduce and reengineer your way to prosperity. You have to increase the revenue line. So what about getting the workers together to do that?

That actually happened at a Harman International Industries plant. At their North Ridge, California, plant, they managed to increase productivity by 30 percent without laying off one of their 6,000 employees—because they used their workers to create and generate ideas to increase revenues. Management figured that they could get by with one-third fewer people and generate much more profit in the short run. But they put their people first, believing that this would provide even greater results than downsizing. They trained people to get jobs elsewhere in the company; they stopped outsourcing many elements; they started producing more components internally; they examined operations and created ways to do things less expensively and with higher quality. As a result, they generated a lot more revenue and created more jobs.

This activity has been very healthy for the firm, giving workers a kind of security that they need to be creative. One idea, for example, was to set up 25 discount stores throughout the country to sell some of the lower-price consumer electronics they make for car radios and computers directly to consumers rather than going through manufacturers.

Share the wealth. Once revenue is increased and profit enhanced, leaders need to share the wealth. Does the fact that senior managers make so much money negatively affect trust? Sure, and these rewards don't have to be the result of a takeover, buyout, or some other one-time deal. Just a few years ago, the average CEO's annual income was 140 times more than that of the average worker. Today it's 200 times more than the average worker. This is obscene, because it creates an "us vs. them" mentality at work rather than promoting teamwork. Now, I don't propose paying everyone the same. However, there are ways of preventing things from getting out of hand. For example, one company I know does not allow its top executives to get a bonus until all the workers are assured a 15 percent increase in their profit sharing.

Can organizations remain competitive when their leaders "put people first" and go for long-term results? Yes, and many companies are proving this.

Get Results. My CEO friend was grumbling again about his favorite topic."With all due respect, Warren, what's missing in your writing and for that matter, most of the other stuff I've read in your field, is the lack of attention to closure." He looked at me as if I were guilty of the most heinous crime. I came back rather lamely and asked him what he meant by "closure," which he had intoned as if it were something sacred. And he said, "I can tell you what I mean in one word: results." Again, that reproachful look. He then ended his denunciation with a final blow, quoting his venerable management guru, Vince Lombardi: "When all is said and done, more is said than done."

My friend was making an important point—one that human resources experts and executives turn to again and again—and that is this relentless emphasis on results. You see, what my friend was really getting at was an area of neglect, something that at times makes us a tad uneasy, even insecure or frustrated: how organizational capabilities and leadership competencies lead to and are connected to desired results.

Many managers focus on organizational capabilities; you know—agile, adaptable, value based mission directed—or on leadership competencies, such as trust, vision, character, and all manner of exemplary attributes, competencies, and capabilities. All well and good, but what is seriously missing is the connection between these critical capabilities and results.

In fact, you can't very well share the wealth if there is not wealth to share. So, we need to keep asking the "so that" question. Yes to "leadership development" so that . . . fill in the result. Yes to "investing in human capital" so that . . . fill in the result. Yes, by all means, yes to "accountability" so that . . . fill in the result. Here is the simple equation that informs virtually every page of this book: *Effective leadership = attributes x results.*

Sounds simple, huh? But many people are not clear on what desired results are or how they are defined and measured. The authors of the book *Results-based Leadership* focus on four areas of results: employee results (human capital), organization results (learning, innovation), customer results (delight target customers), and investor results (cash flow). Every organization needs to learn how to develop and retain "results-based leaders."

Those of us interested in making our organizations more adaptive, effective, creative, and humane are continually asked to justify our existence. We all need to be clear on what we're all about, our raison d'être. We need to seriously address the "so that" questions that usually start or end with "At the end of the day" or the proverbial "bottom line"—those questions practically tattooed on our chests—are one way or another related to the "closure" concern, with how we justify our existence to the enterprise. The very meaning of leadership is inextricably tied to the getting of desired results.

I end with a quote by a famous Zen master. He said "First, enlightenment. Then, the laundry." Leadership is about both.

TRICK #10

Grow Great Groups

Our organizational mythology is out of sync with our reality. We cling to the myth of the omnipotent leader, the larger-than-life individual who can solve every institutional problem, however daunting. We continue to believe in the CEO as corporate Hercules, even as we read cautionary tales almost daily of once-lionized leaders who have failed spectacularly and been replaced after briefer and briefer tenures by angry boards.

All of us who work in business, industry, education, or government observe it and know that, in terms of the organization, the Lone Ranger is dead. The world in which an individual leader, however gifted, however tireless, can save an enterprise single-handedly no longer exists. I suspect that the notion that great institutions are lengthened shadows of individuals has always been an exaggeration, if not a lie—a reflection of our romantic yearning for gods and heroes.

The problems and challenges of corporate life today dwarf any individual, even those as wildly successful as Walt Disney's Michael Eisner or Microsoft's Bill Gates. In a world of increasing globalization and ever-accelerating change, even great leaders are not enough. We need both Great Groups and great leaders, even co-leaders and teams of leaders, if only because, as one wise observer of humanity expressed it, "None of us is as smart as all of us."

Rapid change is breaking the old "chain of command." Bureaucracy—the old structure that still coordinates most industrial, governmental, educational, investigatory, military, religious, and voluntary organizations—consists of a well-defined chain of command, a system of procedures and rules for dealing with all contingencies relating to work, a division of labor based on specialization, promotion and selection based on technical competence, and impersonality in human relations. The bureaucracy was developed as a reaction against the personal subjugation, nepotism, cruelty, and capricious and subjective judgments. Bureaucracy emerged out of the need for order and precision and the individual's demands for impartial treatment. And just as bureaucracy emerged as a creative response to a radically new age, today new shapes are surfacing before our eyes. I see a dramatic change in the philosophy underlying management behavior. This change rises from a new concept of leadership based on increased knowledge of our complex and shifting needs, which replaces an oversimplified, innocent push-button concept of people and organizations; a new concept of power, based on collaboration and reason, which replaces a model of power based on coercion and threat; and a new concept of organization values, based on ideals, which replace the depersonalized, mechanistic value system.

To a large degree, our growing recognition of the need for a new, more collaborative form of leadership results from the emergence of intellectual capital as the most important element in organizational success. In the winning enterprises of an earlier time, the leader could control all the assets. But today's most successful companies live and die according to the quality of their ideas.

Ideas are different from equipment and other physical assets. Ideas are like butterflies—wonderful but elusive. Moreover, the people at the top of the chart have no lock on them. Great ideas can come from anywhere in the enterprise, and they inevitably shift power to those who have them.

Co-author Patricia Ward Biederman and I studied seven extraordinarily successful collaborations for our book, *Organising Genius*. These Great Groups, as we called them, had each changed the world in some significant way. Each had made what Steve Jobs liked to call "a dent in the universe." Disney Feature Animation had created a new art form with Snow White and the Seven Dwarfs. Xerox Corp's Palo Alto Research Center (PARC) and Jobs' Macintosh team at Apple Computer had created the first user-friendly computer. The Manhattan Project had made the atomic bomb, a gadget, as the team called it, that unquestionably changed the world, for better and for worse.

We found that all seven of our Great Groups had important commonalities. Each believed it was on a mission from God. Each was filled with greatly gifted people who wanted to be working on their particular project more than anything else in the world. Each was made up of sometimes delusional optimists—people who did not know the meaning of the word "impossible." Each group believed it was involved in a mortal struggle against a Goliath-like enemy (the Axis powers in the case of the Manhattan Project, IBM for the makers of the Macintosh). Each had become a world unto itself, a place with its own language, jokes, rituals, and, in the case of Apple, its own T-shirts. And, perhaps most telling, each was filled with people having fun.

We also found in these Great Groups a new paradigm for achieving great things—one in which a great leader or leaders devote themselves to unleashing the genius of their colleagues. None of these was a leaderless team. Instead, they constitute a new kind of organization—teams in which each member, including the leader, is needed to create the collective magic.

Whenever I talk about such creative collaborations, I find that people are both exhilarated at the thought of being part of such a group and depressed that their own groups fall so short of the mark. It is no accident that the walls of so many of today's workplaces are decorated with the cynical (albeit hilarious) musings of industry Everyman Dilbert. Too many modern workers regard themselves as wage slaves, and too many workplaces appear to be places of pain, not passion, peopled by individuals who see themselves as underutilized and undervalued.

How can we turn every group into a great one? We have to take a page from the book of the inventors of the PC and other extraordinary innovators and believe that it can be done. Great Groups always have godlike aspirations. Alan Kay, one of the scientists at PARC, recalls that he and his colleagues wanted to achieve far more than they actually did. He, for instance, was trying to develop a laptop computer easy enough for a child to use, more than 20 years before such devices were first produced commercially.

Make Group Membership a Privilege

Life in Great Groups is better. It isn't simply that the work is fascinating and vitally important. The process itself is exciting, even joyous. Something happens in these groups, some alchemy takes place that results, not only in a computer revolution or a new art form, but in a qualitative change in the participants. If only for the duration of the project, people in Great Groups seem to become better than themselves. They see more, achieve more, and have a far better time doing it than they can by working alone.

My coauthor, Patricia Ward Biederman, and I have identified 15 top take-home lessons.

1. Greatness starts with superb people. Recruiting the most talented people possible is the first task. The people who can achieve something unprecedented have talent, intelligence, and originality. They spot the gaps in what we know. They discover and solve problems. They see connections. They have specialized skills, combined with broad interests and multiple frames of reference.

2. Every Great Group has a strong leader. Paradoxically, Great Groups are made up of people with rare gifts working together, and yet there is one person who acts as maestro, organizing the genius of the others. He or she is a pragmatic dreamer, a person with an original but attainable vision. The leader keeps others focused, eliminating distractions, keeping hope alive, and liberating people from the trivial and the arbitrary. Leaders of Great Groups recognize excellence, understand the work, and create the environment to realize it.

3. Great Groups and great leaders create each other. Most nontrivial problems require collective solutions. Collaboration is a necessity. The Lone Ranger, the incarnation of the individual problem solver, is dead. In his place, we have a new model for creative achievement: the Great Group. The heads of Great Groups act decisively, but never arbitrarily. They make decisions without limiting the perceived autonomy of others.

4. The leaders of Great Groups love talent and know where to find it. These leaders are confident enough to recruit people better than themselves. They revel in the talent of others. Where do you find top talent? Sometimes they find you. The talented smell out places that are full of promise and energy, places where the future is being made. The richer the mix of people, the more likely that new connections will be made, new ideas will emerge. Participants know that inclusion is a mark of their own excellence. The real competition is with themselves, to see how good they are and how completely they can use their gifts.

5. Great Groups are full of talented people who can work together. Talent can be so seductive that the person who is recruiting may forget that not every genius works well with others. Certain tasks can only be performed collaboratively. Being amiable, however, is not a prerequisite. Great Groups are tolerant of idiosyncrasies, if only because the members are so focused on the work. Sharing information and advancing the work are the only real social obligations.

6. Great Groups think they are on a mission from God. Great Groups always believe that they are doing something vital, even holy. They are filled with believers, not doubters, and their metaphors are commonly those of war and religion. People know going in that they will be expected to make sacrifices, but they also know they are doing something monumental, something worthy of their best selves. Their clear, collective purpose makes everything they do seem meaningful and valuable.

7. Every Great Group is an island with a bridge to the mainland. Great Groups become their own worlds. They also tend to be physically removed from the world around them. People who are trying to change the world need to be isolated from it, free from its distractions, but able to tap its resources. Participants create a culture of their own with distinctive customs, dress, jokes, even a private language. Such groups treasure their secrets, and have a great deal of fun.

8. Great Groups see themselves as winning underdogs. They inevitably view themselves as the feisty David, hurling fresh ideas at a big, backward-looking Goliath. Much of the gleeful energy of Great Groups stems from this view of themselves as upstarts who will snatch the prize from the fumbling hands of a bigger but less wily competitor.

9. Great Groups always have an enemy. When there is no enemy, you make one up. Why? Because, you can't have a war without one. Whether the enemy occurs in nature or is manufactured, it serves the same purpose. It raises the stakes of the competition, it helps your group rally and define itself. Competition with an outsider seems to boost creativity, but "win-lose" competition within the group reduces it.

10. People in Great Groups have blinders on. People are not distracted by peripheral concerns, even laudable ones such as professional advancement and the quality of their private lives. Great Groups are full of indefatigable people who are struggling to turn a vision into a reality. People in Great Groups fall in love with the project. They are so taken with the beauty and difficulty of the task that they don't want to talk about anything else, be anywhere else, do anything else. They never ask, "How much does it pay?" They ask, "How soon can I start?" and "When can I do it again?"

11. Great Groups are optimistic, not realistic. People in Great Groups believe they can do things no one has ever done. Such groups are often youthful, filled with talented people who have not yet bumped up against their limits or other dispiriting life lessons. They don't yet know what they can't do. Indeed, they're not sure the impossible exists. Optimism is important when people are doing extraordinarily difficult things under pressure.

12. In Great Groups the right person has the right job. The failure to find the right niche for people is why so many workplaces are mediocre, even toxic, in spite of talent. Truly gifted people are never interchangeable. They have unique talents. Such people cannot be forced into roles they are not suited for, nor should they be. Effective leaders allow great people to do the work they were born to do

13. The leaders give people what they need and free them from the rest. Brilliant people want a worthy challenge, a task that allows them to explore their talent, and colleagues who stimulate and challenge them. They don't want trivial duties and obligations and nonessentials. Talented people don't need fancy facilities, but they often do need the right tools—cutting-edge technology for creative collaboration. All Great Groups share information effectively, as members require ideas. Great Groups tend to be places without dress codes, set hours, or other arbitrary regulations. One thing Great Groups do need is protection from bureaucratic meddling. Because Great Groups break new ground, they are more susceptible to being misunderstood, resented, even feared. Civility is the preferred social climate for creative collaboration. Leaders trade the illusion of control that micromanaging gives for the higher satisfactions of orchestrating extraordinary achievement.

14. Great Groups ship. Successful collaborations are dreams with deadlines. They are places of action, not think tanks or retreat centers. Great Groups don't just talk about things, they make things—amazing, original things. Although the members may love the creative process, they know it has to end. Great Groups continue to struggle until the project is brought to conclusion.

15. Great work is its own reward. Great Groups are engaged in solving hard, meaningful problems. The process is difficult but also exhilarating. An urge to explore, to see new relationships, and to turn them into wonderful new things drives these groups. The payoff is not money or glory. Members would do the work for nothing. The reward is the creative process. People ache to do good work. Given a task they believe in and a chance to do it well, they will work tirelessly for no more reward than the one they give themselves.

TRICK #12*

Attract, Retain, and Leverage Talent

Today's leaders must not only have the stature to attract top talent—they must have the character to retain it. Talented people have options. They can walk out the door at any time to go to a competitor or to become a competitor. In this environment, leaders don't automatically command respect. They have to earn it.

One of the leader's primary responsibilities is recruitment. How do you find and keep the right people? It starts with a need for people who can "play together in the sandbox," in the words of Peter Schneider, president of Disney's feature animation studio. That means a sense of compatibility and a willingness to take the work seriously. The team ought to have the right to say who joins, which sometimes means subjecting the recruit to something akin to a hazing experience.

There is also a great deal to be said about self-nomination. People smell out the group that they may want to join. When a certain field gets hot, bright people are drawn almost like iron filings to a magnet. Still, you'll make mistakes, because recruiting is a very chancy game. You can't always predict well, even with the wisdom of a good group.

Beyond recruiting and hiring good people, you need to appreciate the people who are already working for you. Create a culture of respect, caring, and trust and give people a chance to deploy their full talents. The reason people leave an organization once they reach a level of economic sufficiency is because they

* Written with Particia Ward Biederman

want to go to a place where they can use their knowledge and talents and make a greater contribution.

Over the past two decades, the emphasis in business has shifted from maintenance to meaning, from putting in time to making a contribution, from politics to value-added performance, from labor to talent.

What is talent? When I refer to talent, I'm not just talking about performing artists. In business, talent is capability applied to create value that is recognized and rewarded by primary stakeholders—owners, managers, and customers. Those who possess great talent know how their jobs fit within the value chain and not only perform the routine tasks well but also excel at the high-leverage components—tasks that require some degree of proactivity, creativity, initiative, and ingenuity. Talent is wasted whenever it is not recognized, developed, expressed, refined, and leveraged. And my experience suggests that the wholesale waste of talent continues relatively unabated, in spite of technology. To the extent that talent feel like victims, performance suffers proportionately.

Great leaders bring out the best in the talent available to them. They recognize and reward the people who come up with the ideas, make and package the products, sell the products, serve the customers, and support the team. They make each employee feel that he or she plays a vital role and might, through diligence and intelligent application of talents, become indispensable in a here-and-now business sense, meaning that on any given day, his or her presence and performance not only "matters"—it makes all the difference in the world.

Since many managers and leaders are seen as "old dogs" and leading talent is like herding cats, you can expect a few management-talent fights. Don't assume that one reward fits all. No two talents are alike. If you meet one, you meet one. So, rewards should be personalized, based on the preferences and priorities of each individual.

Recruiting (or at least attracting) and keeping top talent is becoming a top priority of leadership. Recruiting and hiring the best people is a crucial factor in the Great Groups. But I don't want to make too much of it because it's not just about recruiting, it's about orchestrating. It isn't just piling up terrific bodies on top of one another. Still, recruiting is important. Great Groups seem to have a rigorous, almost a fraternal or collegial kind of recruiting procedure. As Alan Kay, one of the computer pioneers at Palo Alto Research Center, the R&D center for Xerox Corp., said, "We don't just want a good computer scientist; we want someone who is going to bring fun to us." Or, as Peter Schneider in the Disney group said, "We don't want just another great animator; we want people who can play together in the sandbox." Most of these leaders are connoisseurs of talent. They have a smell, a taste for terrific people. Top performing environments attract top talent. The best talent flows to the best companies to work for. Talent naturally seeks freedom, expression, growth, vision, and mission. The attractions may vary to some degree, but most people of talent seek a supportive environment with capable owners, managers, coaches, cheerleaders, team members, and pay-for-performance systems. They don't want fancy offices and perks and privileges (at first); they value creative freedom and the chance to perform. False promises of security and safety don't cut it.

If you hope to bring future superstars into your organization, I suggest you take a hard look at your hiring process. Before the first interview, review each resume looking for any gaps or red flags that need to be resolved. Identify the values and behaviors of the top performers currently employed by your company to identify critical success factors. The single best predictor of future behavior is past behavior, but what people have done is less important than who they are. To discover who people really are, you may need to conduct multiple interviews, and spend most of the time listening and discerning. Consider your current employees as your best recruiting source as they understand the soul and spirit of your company. Some companies hire 50 percent of all new employees from employee referrals, and it makes for cost-effective recruiting.

Use an assessment tool to benchmark the behavior and values of each potential new hire. Once you develop a benchmark for your company, the accuracy of your hiring will greatly improve. This benchmark will also help reduce employee turnover, increase morale, and solidify your company's position as a market leader. Once you hire a new superstar, welcome this superstar into your company in a way that will accelerate their success. To ensure that each superstar receives the best possible welcome, select a person in your company to mentor the new person in a way that reflects your culture and standards. And, since new people bring fresh perspectives, listen and learn.

How is top talent best retained? In this area of retaining talent, common sense is not common practice. It is easy to cite factors such as a winning program, achievement, stability in the front office, relationship of trust with ownership, collegiality with colleagues, awards, recognition, growth, learning, and money. But personalities and politics complicate matters. Today's leaders must not only have the stature to attract top talent, they must have the character that retains it. Talented people can leave at any time—to go to a competitor or to become one.

But while some say that employee loyalty is dead—thanks in no small part to layoffs, downsizings, reorganizations, mergers and acquisitions—I find that many people are more satisfied with their jobs now, even if their commitment to the organization is less. Hence, no leader can afford to think of employees as disposable commodities. In the Information Age, employees have become not only the company's greatest assets, but also the only sustainable source of competitive advantage.

Today's employees know they need to take more responsibility for their personal and professional development. The new reality has hit, and people are dealing with it. They have a lot of energy for their jobs, but they want more in return. They're offering high-impact performance for rewards that are meaningful to them. So, I suggest that you look at employee loyalty in a different way. Define it by performance rather than time, and seek to enhance that performance in ways that are most meaningful to workers for as long as they decide to stay.

Successful organizations figure out how to align their business goals with each worker's goals. Everyone is looking for a customized solution. Don't assume that what works for one employee will work for another. The time you can invest with an employee to better understand his or her talents and aspirations will pay back tenfold.

How is talent best leveraged? Try a variety of ways: Put top talent with other good talent in teams and give them challenging and meaningful work to do. Make sure this work is valued by the organization and its customers. Give them a special assignment, some "mission impossible" or high-priority project. Pour top talent into products that can be replicated and widely distributed. By creating new products and improving existing products, you gain immense leverage. Seek wide distribution for the work of top talent. If the world-class work of your top talent is poorly promoted and distributed, you gain little leverage. Leverage talent through marketing and sales events. This may mean featuring talent in ads or involving them in sales in some way. Make your top talent bigger than life. Create an image and identity for them. Invest wisely in advertising and public and media relations. Consider making a brand of the talent's name. Engage willing, mature talent in the high-leverage activities of mentoring, modeling, and coaching up-and-coming talent.

What is the new role of managers and leaders? Like management in the sports and entertainment worlds, the primary role of management is to support, discipline, and leverage the talent. Support suggests providing service and removing obstacles. The leader often asks four questions: How is it going? What are you learning? What are your goals now in light of how it is going and what you are learning; and How can I help you? In this way, the leader avoids owning the problem and yet offers himself or herself as a source of help.

The leader's role is to unleash talent by creating conditions of trust, setting up performance agreements, and then holding people accountable. The best leaders are masters of making things happen. They build energy by creating compelling visions and then unleashing talent. Harold A. Poling, former chairman and CEO of Ford Motor Company, said, "One stepping stone to a world-class organization is to tap into the creative and intellectual power of each employee." Leaders give their people the time, support, and tools they need to stimulate creative thinking. At 3M employees are encouraged to develop new products, even build their own businesses within the company. Those who succeed are given promotions and pay raises. There is no penalty for those who fail. Knowing that people are energized by the chance to see their ideas come to fruition, Percy Barnevik, CEO of the 215,000-employee conglomerate ABB (Asea Brown Boveri Ltd), in Switzerland, created 5,000 separate "profit centers," each having no more than 50 employees, to achieve increased responsibility, authority, and recognition.

Great leaders inspire people to do great work. They delegate responsibility and the authority needed to get a job done—unleashing tremendous energy. Employees want to feel that they are trusted and valued. Nothing pumps up an employee's energy more quickly or completely than when he or she is supported for showing personal initiative or calculated risk-taking.

Increasingly, managers are becoming coaches, colleagues, and cheerleaders for the employees they support rather than prison wardens or executioners. The best managers allow their employees to make mistakes or to disagree with no fear of retribution.

Training and development are highly valued by today's younger workers who constantly want to learn new skills, both to keep the job exciting and challenging as well as to increase their marketability. The workplace is full of an abundance of opportunities. Ask people what they want to do, pair them with the right people and positions, and the results are amazing. "In the industrial age, the CEO sat on the top of the hierarchy and didn't have to listen to anybody," says John Scully, former CEO of Apple Computer Co. "In the information age, you have to listen to the ideas of all people in the organization."

In his book, *Post Capitalist Society,* management expert Peter Drucker states that each employee must be asked: "What should we hold you accountable for? What information do you need? And, in turn, what information do you owe the rest of us? Each worker has to participate in decisions as to what equipment is needed; how the work should be scheduled; indeed what the basic policy of the entire company should be."

Leaders communicate with employees openly. Jack Welch, CEO of General Electric Co., relishes in his face-to-face sessions at GE's training center where he takes on the roles of coach, teacher, and mentor—listening, lecturing and above all, interacting with his managers. These sessions reinforce the informality and atmosphere of trust and camaraderie GE is trying to instill—and encourage employees to open their minds and challenge themselves.

To leverage the talent you have—and to make sure you have the talent you will need in the future—create supportive work environments that foster employee creativity, innovation, and fun. Southwest Airlines is an organization that dares to unleash the imagination and energy of its people by making work fun. Southwest reinvented air travel 25 years ago with its low fares and zany irreverent style. They have made flying an event. They keep costs low, productivity high. They have the courage to be "real people" who love and care at work and celebrate often.

Workers often complain that they get paid the same whether they work hard or just punch the clock. They have no sense of ownership and very little loyalty. Enlightened executives explore stock options and profit sharing, and before there's any significant salary increases for the top brass, they make sure that workers receive a share. They understand that motivated workers make better workers.

In an environment of massive inequality in compensation, how can you attract and keep the best people? Well, you probably won't unless you restructure your compensation, taking a very hard look at the top people in the organization.

In today's world, you need the internal security to hire people who are better than you are. If you are insecure, you will be threatened by competence below you.

If you feel stuck, I think you should talk with the boss directly, one-on-one. And if that doesn't work, go around and talk to other people and maybe even to the boss's boss. And if that does not work, you have to leave. Is it cavalier or callous of me to recommend that? In the long run that business is going to fail if it doesn't change its ways, so the end result is the same.

It's like staying in a bad marriage because you're frightened by the prospect of being too old to remarry and not being in a financial position to strike out on your own again. So you stuff it all down and say, I'm going to stay in a lousy relationship because the alternatives are worse. Often, the alternatives are better if you act on them.

TRICK #13

Lead Teams to Greatness

For two decades now, I have been writing about leadership. But, earlier in my career, I was interested in the dynamics of small groups. I did some research on the interaction between leaders and followers in groups.

Has my thinking changed? Not really. I would say what has changed is the leadership required in organizations. It's a different mode of leadership. The Lone Ranger is dead. When *The Economist* magazine recently asked approximately 180 leaders what the major influence on future organizations would be, two-thirds of them said it would be teams and groups.

Clearly, the John Wayne model of leadership won't work. What's needed now is a different kind of leadership. People who think they can do it by themselves are nuts. Yet we still have the cult of the CEOs. We enshrine them, and probably celebrate them too much. But I think that's partly an American phenomenon. When working in Europe recently, I kept hearing reactions against having these icons and this canonization of leadership.

Groups, teams, communities, partnerships, stakeholders, colleagues, collaborators signal the end of the "Great Man," the death of the John Wayne myth.

FOUR FACTORS

I see four factors having influence in bringing groups to their current prominence—reasons why the signature of the 21st century organization will be teams, networks, and groups.

1. Participative management. The least important influence in regard to fostering communities of practice, partnership, and great groups is participative management. It plays a role, but it may be the least important.

2. The rapidity and complexity of change driven by globalization and technology. Thats obvious to anybody who has been alive for the last five years. We live in the topsy-turvy world of technology and globalization. (I will say more on this in Trick #16.)

3. Seismic shifts in the geopolitical landscape. At a more macro level, the world is in a tizzy. Nobody can tell what's going to happen. As one CEO put it , "If you're not confused, you don't know what's going on." I see two dangerous things going on simultaneously: On the one hand, you've got a descending great power, Russia. Any country that's losing its collective self-esteem is always dangerous. And on the other hand, you've got China, an ascending power, dangerous because of its notions about how it'll achieve greatness. So when you have one great power declining and one great power emerging, you've got an incredibly turbulent world. A case of collective vertigo is hitting everybody right now.

4. On the personal dimension, more people are feeling alone, disaffiliated, disenfranchised, anxious, and often dyspeptic. In his article "Bowling Alone," Robert D. Putnam noted that now more people are sporting alone, not in leagues. He visited a lot of bowling alleys and discovered people there in the afternoons and evenings bowling alone, a sort of heightened form of alienation. He looked at voting records, membership in voluntary associations—from the PTA to political associations to Boy Scout troops—and saw a sharp decline in participation.

Well, given all that churning and uncertainty, it's becoming necessary to find our way by "bowling together." As I wrote in *Organizing Genius*, none of us is as smart as all of us. So empowerment and participative management are hard necessities. We need groups and teams—aside from their animating brainpower—to survive in what is a lonelier and more distancing world. Technology can either contribute to this feeling of alienation or work to foster collaboration. When we talk about disintermediation, we are really describing the techies who are just working alone, at home. When I go to Starbucks in the morning, I see all these techies there to have some form of human intercourse. As we disintermediate ourselves away from working with other people and do everything alone—even bowl alone—we have a correlative need to work together and to feel the warmth of human communication.

While there are plenty of discussion groups on the Internet, and you can stay in contact with people all over the world easily with e-mail, I don't think you can create a new community without meaningful human interaction where people really get to know each other. I think e-mail helps to fill in when we can't be together and facilitate times when we can be together.

Great Groups foster great leaders. All great groups of self-managed teams have great leadership, but creating the social architecture for self-managed teams takes a different leadership. It isn't that we're absent leadership, it's that we're no longer stuck in the macho command-and-control mode.

The subtlety and nuance required to create a climate that nurtures a Great Group or a great culture take more exquisite skills of leadership than ever before.

I don't believe in this thing called "self-managed groups." I think they are groups that have a lot of autonomy and sense of responsibility, that they are terrific, but I do think a leader is needed to create that culture.

I suggest that if you want to organize genius and have a great group, you must learn the fine art of "herding cats." Some leaders—among them Steve Jobs, Walt Disney, Kelly Johnson at Lockheed's Skunk Works, and John Andrew Rice at Black Mountain College—didn't have great people skills. In fact, they herded their cats with whips; and yet they produced phenomenal results. Leaders typically provide direction and meaning that resonate in the heart and soul and mind. But many leaders of great groups are abrasive, if not downright arrogant.

These people are all alchemists. They are creating something out of nothing. They are creating something magical. They are creating an object of enchantment. And when you're playing for mortal stakes, when you think you're involved in a group that's going to change the world, you can be a son-of-a-bitch for a time.

If you can create a group that thinks they can "make a dent in the universe," as Steve Jobs told the team that created the

Macintosh computer, one's personal foibles, losing one's temper, one's style become less important. When you feel transported, and you're part of the excitement and thrill and the electrifying feeling of doing something that nobody has ever done before, arrogance can be excused.

But most leaders develop great people leadership qualities over time. Steve Jobs, founder of Apple Computers, got a lot better as he grew and became seasoned. And the present leader of Disney Feature Animation Studio, Peter Schneider, has all of the intuitive qualities of a leader.

But would the money spent on trying to develop managers' soft skills be better spent elsewhere? Absolutely not. I don't like the phrase "soft skills." I think these are the hardest skills to learn. They are the things that will make the biggest difference in organizations.

Bob Haas, CEO of Levi Strauss, has said the hard skills are not getting the pants out the door. The hard skills are creating the work force that will be motivated to be productive. So, the soft skills are the hardest skills. Those so-called "soft" skills are going to be more important.

The truly creative collaborations seem like miracles, but companies can replicate them by applying the "take-home lessons" provided by extraordinary groups. Exceptional, exemplary leaders have a vision of what's possible.

A certain exhilaration comes with creating an Apple Computer, a *Snow White*, a bomb you think will save western civilization. But most of us don't work in organizations with such clear, sexy missions. Sometimes I feel that I'm talking to clinically depressed groups. Someone once said, "You know, Warren, you talk about these marvelous groups, but I work in the city government, and it isn't exactly exciting."

When I hear such comments, I think about companies like Springfield Remanufacturing, where they remanufacture diesel engines. A dirtier, less glamorous job you probably couldn't come up with. But the people are genuinely excited about their work because they know exactly how what they do contributes to the company and the community.

When I ask audiences, "How many of you people have been in Great Groups?" most people raise their hands. But usually it's been just one or two situations and often it was temporary sometimes at work, or it was a play, an athletic team, a political campaign, or a research project.

I know in my own case, I've been in three or four Great Groups in my lifetime, and those were pretty heady experiences. But I think we can have a lot more of them if we pay attention.

I don't think that you have to be young, male, and willing to give everything for the cause—to be part of a great group. But I think the heat of these groups makes it difficult to stay in that atmosphere too long. There is something about what it takes out of you. It is a Faustian bargain: you really are giving up a lot. But I think you can't get repotted and revitalized in another Great Group.

Another characteristic of Great Groups is the necessity for optimism or the inability to see that this mission can't be done. Steve Jobs talks about cultivating a beginner's mind. I think that's possible. I like to think that I walk through life with my eyebrows continually raised.

I think back to many of my mentors who were innocent and curious people. People like Abe Maslow and Doug McGregor, just to take two, were extraordinarily curious people until their end.

These leaders were purveyors of hope who created a suspension of disbelief. They didn't know some things couldn't be done. Someone once said about the composer Saint-Saens: "He knew everything; all he lacked was inexperience." I think you've got to have a sense of wonder and hope.

TRICK #14

Create Your Own Great Group

How do you create a Great Group? The leader makes the group, and the group makes the leader. I realized this truth as a young man in World War II. I was what was called a replacement officer. It was right after the Battle of the Bulge—in December 1944—and I was a green platoon leader in the infantry. But my platoon guys—all experienced veterans—helped train me, a 19-year-old second lieutenant just out of Fort Benning, to become their leader. They taught me everything from how to hit the ground and dig a foxhole to how to make a decent meal out of C rations and direct my scouts. They taught me all the ropes. They wanted me to lead them, and they made it possible for me to do that. I was obviously scared to death at what I was thrust into, but they made me into something beyond my dreams. That was a Great Group.

Of course, I knew some things they didn't know. I had just gone through four months of advanced military training, and I was able to impart some things about strategy. I could give them some sense of perspective about where we were and where the war was going—a glimpse of the big picture—and that gave them an idea of when we were going to be relieved, which was very important.

And I gave them a sense of confidence, which is paradoxical, given the fact that I joined the platoon without any real experience. Yet, somehow or other, they gave me the confidence, and then later I gave them the confidence. I think we both realized that we were playing for mortal stakes and that in a morbid sense, our fates were interrelated.

Today, we need to take such battlefield experience and apply it to the office and factory to make service groups succeed. But, the question is how? How do you take the experiences and lessons of extraordinary groups and apply them to ordinary organizations?

Great Groups are vivid Utopias. They are pictures of the way organizations ought to look—a set of aspirations and a graphic illustration of what's possible. So how do we, in our mundane organizations, create these things? I think there are many factors that we can look at. Perhaps the key factor is finding meaning in what you do. How do you make people feel that what they're doing is somewhat equivalent to a search for the Holy Grail? This is more than just having a vision. The vision must have a deep meaning. It has to have some connection with changing the world, with a mission from God.

A Great Group must have not only a meaningful vision but also the ability to seize opportunities to fulfill that vision. How it pulls that off is something of a mystery. Many groups are, in a sense, closed entities, and yet they are somehow in touch with the market. On one hand, these groups are self-contained island communities. On the other, they have antennae that extend to the outside.

For example, J. Robert Oppenheimer, the creative force behind the Manhattan Project, knew where to find the best young physicists to develop the atomic bomb. So, although he was in Los Alamos, and God knows that was a woebegone place, he was able to recruit many of the best minds available. He had a Rolodex in his head long before the actual device was invented. Many Great Groups are enclosed and protected, yet also have the networks to know what's going on in the "real" world.

Many of the things that emerge from these groups are radical departures. You may have a group that is isolated, doing what it thinks may be a remarkable breakthrough, but, in fact, it has no resonance with the market, has no connection with what the needs or interests of people are. This is where there's a lot of luck involved. It is also where leadership counts.

A leader is needed to protect the group from disruptive outside forces yet possess a sort of proverbial Rolodex in the sky to know what's going on. Real leaders are able to recruit their troops and protect them from the "suits," or what they used to call "toner heads" at Xerox, and also have a strong connection with the outside world. They keep the bureaucrats away from the creativity going on.

A Great Group has a creative leader who is also a protector—who somehow gets the money or protects the money from other departments or fiefdoms. In a Great Group, you always have to have some patrician in the background who can talk to the suits. Leaders, whether filling one of these roles or both, are rarely the brightest people in the group. Rather, they have extraordinary taste, which makes them more curators than creators. They appreciate talent and nurture talent, and they have the ability to recognize valuable ideas. Leaders are almost like midwives of ideas. They understand what is going on. When you come to them with an idea, they aren't going to say, "Well, that's nice," but instead "Maybe we can use that."

The leader's function is to find the link to the market. The leader is the person who goes to the outside world, who brings to an audience of executives the work of the creative genius in the group. He is the salesman, translator, facilitator between the group's genius and the market. He sells the dream to the people who aren't close to it

Leaders often fill the gap that others may not be filling at a particular time. That means being able to move into different roles—and having the capacity to abandon ego to the talents of others. They create a space and a role for the best use of their talents. These leaders may be underappreciated by the world but fully acknowledged within the company. They are keen listeners, supportive, protectors of dreams, guardians of the group's meaning.

Why do people respond to them? These leaders are the incarnation of the dream, of a form of excellence, of what makes that group great. And you want to live up to that ideal. Leaders provide direction and meaning; they generate and sustain trust; they are purveyors of hope, they get results. Their personalities vary enormously, but they have an incredible sense of spotting talent. They find people who can do things that they can't.

But they are not permissive. They have a sense of measures and milestones, deadlines and clear metrics—and they keep those in front of the group. With monotonous regularity, the leader reminds people of what's important. If the group doesn't produce by a certain date, then some competitor will do this before us.

There's always got to be that haunting sense of a deadline. These are fiercely competitive groups, and the only way they can be fiercely competitive is knowing there's a deadline. Great Groups have to ship product.

If you are sailing into uncharted territory, you may not know what the metrics should be. The notion that you could do something that no one else has done is almost unwarranted optimism. They must have an innocence about them—they can't know it can't be done. Youth is often important here, because they don't know what they don't know. Great Groups are very special. They encourage us to aspire to be something more than we are. You are aware of what can happen when you are part of a group that makes a difference, rather than the humdrum, boring, drifting organization we see too often.

It's hard to imagine a large organization with hundreds of hives of Great Groups. But the lessons here about leadership, meaning, recruiting, and protection of intellectual capital are terribly important. There's a certain intensity in these groups. When you walk into a particular company, you can recognize whether it's happening there or not.

All of us have been members, at one time in our lives at least, of a terrific group, one in which we never felt more creative and alive. Invariably, the leader has this charisma or sense of letting go, or has the talent to bring in many good people. You too can do this. I'm convinced that these groups not only can be created within Fortune 1000 companies but sustained, if we ask, "What are we doing here together? What are we trying to produce? What has meaning for us? What will keep us motivated? Let's take a look at our leadership. Let's take a look at whether we have any moments of honoring or celebrating our achievements. Let's take a look at our metrics."

In many ways, you can get groups to be reflective about their shortcomings and the things they could do to make themselves, if not great, a lot better than they now are. Executives often ask me about sharing their knowledge with the troops, giving them a sense of the big picture. "How much knowledge should I reveal? How much should I hold back?" I tell them, "You should reveal as much as possible, but without scaring people."

What I learned as a university president was that you can't always talk about your own insecurities. You can't talk about all the perceived difficulties that you might see, by virtue of your position, and that the others can't see. You don't want to share things that will diminish the enthusiasm. People may not believe that their leaders are omniscient, but they have a certain stake in thinking that a leader has enough security to guide them through treacherous waters. Leaders of Great Groups share perspective, providing a sense of destiny as well as an awareness of the forces they are up against. Every Great Group invents or creates an enemy to preserve that cohesiveness and sense of elan. If you have a budget shortage and you're not getting the help you need, you may want to indicate, "Well, we're going to have to do the best we can, given the budgets we're getting from headquarters," and just go with it that way.

So, if you can't find a Great Group to join, create one.

TRICK #15*

Learn the Secrets of
Creative Collaboration

Great groups have shaped our world, from the gathering of
young geniuses at Los Alamos who unleashed the atom, to the
youthful scientist and hackers who invented a computer what
was personal as well as powerful. That should hardly surprise us.
In a society as complex and technologically sophisticated as ours,
the most urgent projects require the coordinated contributions of
many talented people. Whether the task is building a global
business or discovering the mysteries of the human brain, one
person can't hope to accomplish it, however gifted or energetic
he or she may be. And yet, even as we make the case for collaboration, we resist the idea of collective creativity. Our mythology
refuses to catch up with our reality. And so we cling to the myth
of the Lone Ranger, the romantic idea that great things are usually accomplished by a larger-than-life individual working alone.

   Given our continuing obsession with solitary genius, reflected
in everything from the worship of film directors to our fascina-
tion with Bill Gates and other high-profile entrepreneurs, it is no
surprise that we tend to underestimate just how much creative
work is accomplished by groups. Today an important scientific
paper may represent the best thinking and patient lab work of
hundreds of people. Collaboration constantly takes place in the
arts as well. A classic example is the Michelangelo masterpiece,
the ceiling of the Sistine Chapel. In our mind's eye, we see
Michelangelo, looking remarkably like Charlton Heston, labor-
ing alone on the scaffolding high above the chapel floor. In fact,

* Written with Particia Ward Biederman

93

13 people helped paint the work. Michelangelo was not only an artist; he was, as biographer William E. Wallace points out, the head of a good-sized entrepreneurial enterprise.

We must turn to Great Groups if we hope to begin to understand how that rarest of precious resources—genius—can be successfully combined with great effort to achieve results that enhance all our lives. It is in such groups that we may also discover why some organizations seem to breed greatness, freeing members to do better than anyone imagined they could be.

All Great Groups have extraordinary leaders. It's a paradox, really, because Great Groups tend to be collegial and nonhierarchical, peopled by singularly competent individuals who often have an anti-authoritarian streak. Nonetheless, virtually every Great Group has a strong and visionary head. First off, each leader has a keen eye for talent. Recruiting the right genius for the job is the first step in building many great collaborations. The aim of group leaders is almost always one of greatness, not simply an ambition to succeed. The dream is the engine that drives the group, the vision that inspires the team to work as if the fate of civilization rested on their completing their project.

Many great groups have a dual administration. They have a visionary leader, and they have someone who protects them from the outside world. Great Groups tend to be nonconformist. People in them are always rule busters, never insiders or corporate types on the fast track. People in great groups are always on their own track. As a result, they often need someone to deflect not just the criticism but even the attention of the bureaucrats and conventional thinkers elsewhere in the organization. The protectors typically lack the glamour of the visionary leaders, but they are no less essential, particularly in enterprises that require official sanction or that cannot realize their dream without institutional consent.

Who becomes part of a great group? If not out-and-out rebels, participants may lack traditional credentials or exist on the margins of their professions. They are almost always young. Probably the most important thing that young members bring is their often delusional confidence. Thus, many great groups are fueled by an invigorating, completely unrealistic view of what they can accomplish. Not knowing what they can't do puts everything in the realm of the possible. Great Groups often show evidence of collective denial. And "Denial ain't just a river in Egypt," as 12-steppers like to say. Denial can obscure obstacles and stiffen resolve. It can liberate. Great groups are not realistic. They are exuberant and irrationally optimistic.

Many of the people in Great Groups are tinkerers. There's a joke about engineers that captures the spirit of many participants in creative collaborations: An engineer meets a frog, who offers the engineer anything he wants if he will kiss the frog. "No," says the engineer. "Come on," says the frog. "Kiss me, and I'll turn into a beautiful women." "Nah," says the engineer. "I don't have time for a girlfriend . . . but a talking frog, that's really neat."

Curiosity fuels every Great Group. The members don't simply solve problems. They are engaged in a process of discovery that is its own reward. Many of the people in these groups have dazzling individual skills. But they also have another quality that allows them both to identify significant problems and to find creative, boundary-busting solutions rather than simplistic ones: they are hungry, urgent minds.

Virtually every Great Group defines itself in terms of an enemy. Sometimes the enemy is real, as the Axis powers were for the Manhattan Project. But more often, the chief function of the enemy is to solidify and define the group itself. In great groups the engagement of the enemy is both dead serious and a lark. Great groups always see themselves as winning underdogs, wily Davids toppling the bloated Goliaths of tradition and convention.

People in great groups often seem to have struck a Faustian bargain, giving up their normal lives, if not their souls, in exchange for greatness. Because they are mission maniacs, obsessed with the project at hand, relationships outside the groups routinely suffer.

Although Great Groups experience their moments of near despair, they are more often raucous with laughter. Creative collaborators become members of their own tribe, with their own language, in-jokes, dress, and traditions.

Great Groups often fall apart when the project is finished. Why do these often short-lived associations burn so bright in the memories of former members? There are a host of reasons. Life in the group is often the most fun members ever have. They revel in the pleasure that comes from exercising all their wits in the company of people "used to dealing lightning with both hands," as one great-group member put it. Communities based on merit and passion are rare, and people who have been in them never forget them. And then there is the sheer exhilaration of performing greatly. Talent wants—and needs—to exercise itself.

People pay a price for their membership in Great Groups. Postpartum depression is often fierce, and the intensity of collaboration is a potent drug that may make everything else, including everything after, seem drab and ordinary.

But no one who has participated in one of these adventures in creativity and community seems to have any real regrets. How much better to be with other worthy people, doing worthy things, than to labor alone. In a Great Group you are liberated for a time from the prison of self. As part of the team, you are on leave from the mundane—no questions asked—with its meager rewards and sometimes onerous obligations. Genius is rare, and the chance to exercise it in a dance with others is rarer still. Karl Wallenda, the legendary tightrope walker, once said, "Being on the tightrope is living; everything else is waiting." Most of us wait. In great groups talent comes alive.

None of Us Is As Smart As All of Us

None of us is as smart as all of us. With poetic economy, it summed up so much of what we discovered when we looked at remarkable creative collaborations.

The groups we studied were as disparate as the Walt Disney studio, which invented the animated feature, and the Manhattan Project, which gave the world, for better and for worse, the first atomic bomb. They included both Lockheed Skunk Works, which pioneered the stealth technology deployed so dramatically in the Persian Gulf War, and Black Mountain College, a tiny, groudbreaking arts school that flourished for a time in the foothills of the Blue Ridge Mountains. Each of the seven exemplifies the power of a group of gifted people inspired by a worthy cause and creatively led to accomplish more than any one person could hope to do. Each of our seven groups had set out to change the world in some fundamental way: "to put a dent in the universe," as Steve Jobs liked to say when extolling his Macintosh group at Apple. And although each group had succeeded in its own way, all seven had striking commonalities as well.

For all we talk of teams and teamwork, we still cling to the notion of the individual hero, the Hercules who can do anything and do it all by himself. We still tend to think of our institutions as lengthened shadows of a Great Man or Great Woman. The myth was probably never true: And the myth certainly isn't true today. The time is long past when one person can know, let alone do, everything, as Thomas Jefferson came close to doing. Even a Leonardo da Vinci would be overwhelmed by a world such as ours in which, every day, our problems become more complex, our interactions become more global, and a constantly changing technology accelerates the rate of change. In today's world, one is too small a number to produce greatness. The most important enterprises and most urgent projects require teams of talented people, working together toward a common goal under leadership that does whatever it takes to unleash that talent and get the job done.

STRONG LEADERSHIP

Although our Great Groups were packed with talented people, most with healthy egos, none was a democracy, collective, or leaderless team. Each had a strong leader or, in some cases, a pair of leaders who facilitated the work of the group. In almost every case, the leader's first and most important responsibility was recruitment. To some extent, every Great Group is a miracle, a triumph of talent and luck over the principle of regression to the mean. But no Great Group is even possible without a critical mass of talent; the leaders of all successful collaborations know this. Bob Taylor, the superb manager who led Xerox PARC in the 1970's, used to say "You can't pile together enough good people to make a great one."

The leaders of Great Groups worship talent, and they know where to find it. It's as if they were born with great Rolodexes in their heads. Even before every university had a computer science department, Bob Taylor knew who was doing the most exciting research in the nascent field because he had evaluated grant proposals as head of the U. S. Advanced Research Projects Agency, later DARPA. When J. Robert Oppenheimer went searching for the greatest physicists in the free world, he knew where to begin because the best and the brightest had gathered regularly at international conferences instituted by Danish Nobelist Niels Bohr.

The process continues today, and top universities such as Stanford are at the heart of it. Some Silicon Valley companies depend on Stanford teaching assistants to point them to the next generation of software greats. Bill Labs, as some wags call the high-powered R&D operation Bill Gates has put together at Microsoft, has recruited so many top professors that one observer e-mailed a colleague "Last one in academe, turn out the lights."

While the leaders of Great Groups love talent, they also know that not everyone is capable of collaborating.

To be successful collaborators, people don't have to be pleasant in the conventional sense: Young Richard Feynmann was sometimes downright rude at Los Alamos, but his ideas more than compensated for any social discomfort he caused. But all participants have to be on the same mission and able to interact in ways that advance their common goal, not detract from it.

Once the leader has brought the group together, he or she has to make it work, which is not as easy as it sounds. One of the paradoxes of Great Groups is that they are routinely made up of people who are smarter than the leader. Often, the participants must identify the specific problems to be solved as well as find solutions for them.

The leader of such a group exercises his or her creativity by unleashing it in others, by allowing them to sing and dance, as a Xerox official put it. The leader makes the achievement possible and soars on their wings.

DEALING WITH THE "ENEMY"

One key responsibility of such a leader is to keep away the bureaucrats—the "suits." General Leslie Groves had a genius for keeping the U.S. Army from meddling in the work of the scientists at Los Alamos, a critical element in their success that few scientists gave him credit for. This often requires real talent on the leader's part because, by definition, Great Groups are engaged in groundbreaking work, and the truly original can be awfully threatening to an organization's bottom-liners.

Conversely, the leader must also be able to work with the bureaucrats to get the group's product out the door. Great Groups aren't think tanks, although they hum with new ideas. They produce things. The leader must be able to sell the organization on the viability of the product.

People who lead genius have assorted other responsibilities as well. They must find ways to get critical information from one person to another, a task exponentially more difficult before e-mail. Taylor did it by having mandatory weekly meetings (the beanbag chairs on which everyone sprawled have become the stuff of legend). He also had a masterful way of diffusing conflict. Instead of allowing people who disagreed to have the verbal equivalent of a fist fight, he urged that each get to the point where he or she could articulate the other's position. (The Iroquois Indians had a similar method for resolving conflict.) One of the virtues of this approach is that it enhances collegiality instead of exacerbating the tendency of teammates who disagree to think of themselves as on opposite sides—us against them. Creativity thrives when the enemy is on the outside, not in the cubicle next door.

Great Groups always have an enemy. The mindset typical of members of Great Groups is that of the feisty underdog, plucky little David taking on a bloated, overblown, anachronistic Goliath. At Apple, IBM was the enemy. During Bill Clinton's 1992 campaign for the U. S. presidency, the enemy was the Republican establishment that failed to represent the interests of the little guy.

Turning a project into a war always ratchets up the stakes and energizes the participants. In the corridors of Coca-Cola, the real mantra is not the feel-good advertising slogan of the moment but "Destroy Pepsi." At McDonald's, the role of the great Satan is assigned to Burger King. Late last year, when Burger King announced it had improved its recipe so that it now had America's greatest french fries, McDonald's prepared to bomb its rival back to the Stone Age. McDonald's vice chair Jack Greenburg sent a memo to every McDonald's owner and operator in the U. S. Included in the call to arms: "The most powerful weapon we have in our arsenal is for our restaurants to deliver hot, fresh, great-tasting fries. We're operating from a position of strength with the product, the people, and the plan it takes to win. If we do this right and keep our eyes on the fries, we will win this battle and make significant headway in the war as well."

Great Groups crackle with excitement. No one needs to be told to work harder because everyone is addicted to the work. The people in these alliances have a cause they believe in, comrades whom they respect, and brains full of the feel-good chemicals released by problem solving. They are happy campers, telling inside jokes and creating rituals peculiar to their tribe (although their neglected pets and loved ones may be considerably less happy). In memory, it will always have been the best of times.

One trait common to all our groups was an almost delusional optimism. They didn't believe there was anything they couldn't do. Time has a way of teaching people their limitations, which may be why so many participants in Great Groups are young. According to psychologist Martin Seligman, realism is a risk factor for depression, with all its attendant ills, including the inability to act. Great Groups are confident to the point of chutzpah. They don't know what failure means. As director John Frankenheimer recalls of the early days of live TV, when he collaborated on classic dramas, "We didn't know we couldn't do it, so we did it."

TRICK #16

Cope with Speed and Complexity (Raplexity)

I think that the problems facing executives, whether they be in large or small organizations, are related to the speed at which issues hit them, and the complexity of those issues. I use the word *raplexity* to signify rapidity and complexity.

Information and communication technology will change not just the degree but also the kind of leadership that we're going to need. Because, as we democratize the workplace and as we develop the kinds of technologies and digital interactivity that we are now seeing, our communication is going to become more, should I say, rampant. We will be able to talk simultaneously to a lot more people than we ever thought possible. And we are going to have a lot more information at our fingertips. This will democratize the workplace even more.

This means that leaders are going to have to be very comfortable with advanced technology and the changes that it's going to bring. Many of them aren't. I have a board in my leadership institute, made up of very terrific leaders, and they all have e-mail. But when I asked how many of them use it, only half of the hands went up, and some of those went up rather lamely. Rather haltingly.

I think that information technology will have profound consequences for how we organize in the future, and also for the sophistication that will be required by those of us who are leaders. The younger generation has been brought up in a high-tech world. I was born at a time when television was unheard of, when FM radio was virtually unheard of.

What will this mean for tomorrow's leaders? Let me draw an analogy. It's sort of like psychiatry and psychopharmacology. My wife is a psycho pharmacologist. She was trained as a psychiatrist, but she realized that talk therapy wasn't enough. And that many mental health problems can be dealt with effectively through medication and pharmaceuticals. But she realized that both are necessary. She still does talk therapy, but she also uses medication.

In a similar way, leaders are going to have to be both comfortable with advanced technology but at the same time probably even more hands-on than ever before. They will need more interpersonal competence.

What Executives Can Do

What can you do to keep pace with the 'raplexity' and merit the incentive compensation you desire? Well, I suggest that you do three things.

1. Seek feedback. Arrange within your team, group, or family some form of "reflective backtalk." I learned this lesson when talking to one CEO who said: "I talk to my spouse for reflective backtalk, and I use her as a mirror. She acts as a psychological safety net." We all need to reflect on our experience, particularly negative experience, with someone we trust.

2. Keep a diary or journal. Record your reflections on your life experience in a journal. You will find this simple practice to be invaluable in your quest for wisdom.

3. Read a few biographies and other books authored by your mentors. You don't need a psychotherapist. Just look for inspiring examples—stories of successful people with whom you can relate. Make these people your models and mentors. Learn what you can from their inspiring examples and writings.

What Organizations Can Do

Organizations can do 10 simple things to help people cope with "raplexity."

1. Keep learning. Send people to the best courses at the best universities and training companies. Make sure this learning is relevant and is applied on the job.

2. Make changes in the organization to make it easy for people to grow. Don't send a changed person back into an unchanged organization.

3. Start coaching. Identify people who are known to be good coaches and mentors and make them available and visible. If you walk around and ask: Who are the people here who have coached or mentored good leaders?, you will get answers.

4. Make it okay to tell the truth. Encourage your mentors and others who supply you with feedback to speak up, to "speak truth to power."

5. Reward the straight shooters. The major reason why people don't speak truth to those in power is the history of the messenger being shot.

6. Provide diverse experience within the organization. Some of the best leaders I know of are people like the *Washington Post's* Ben Bradlee who have had a wide range of experience in the business. Ben, for example, has worked in production, reporting, editing, managing, and leading. In the best organizations, every senior executive spends substantial time in research, sales, manufacturing, marketing, management, and leadership assignments—so that they have a prismatic view.

7. Give people more international assignments. Many executives have to be convinced, almost coerced, to take an international assignment and be exposed to different languages and cultures. But you can't get a clear idea of how the world is changing just by talking to customers over the phone.

8. Keep people surprised. Senior executives, especially need to be surprised, even shocked, occasionally. Bertrand Russell, when asked about his favorite student, said: "He's my favorite because he always looks puzzled." All you can tell people is to keep their eyes open, embrace ambiguity, and not be frightened of surprise. One of my favorite questions to executives is: "In your company, what's the mean time between surprises?" How do you get people to improvise? Today, you must like the sound of jazz, and the sound of surprise.

9. Make sure your name stays in the phone book. The most important thing you could know about your business future is whether or not your name is still in the phone book. If it's not, you are probably out of business.

10. Prize both masculine and feminine leadership attributes. I agree that attributes more commonly associated with women will be in high demand among leaders in the next decade. But I hesitate to say that women leaders will be more in demand, because I don't want anyone to steal the female side of me. Many of the male leaders I admire give full expression to their feminine sides. In fact, some male leaders are almost bisexual in their ability to be open and reflective. Frankly, I don't believe that gender is the determining factor in leadership. What counts is the ability to be both tough and tender as the situation dictates.

Exemplary Leadership

Exemplary leadership is what I call leadership that results in creative, intelligent, and competitive organizations. I use the word *exemplary* very carefully. It comes out of 13th century English, and it means to "clear the woods," or to "clear the way." We're talking about pathfinders. We can learn much by examining extraordinary organizations and exemplary people.

Let me use two cartoons to further illustrate exemplary leadership. The first one, a Charles Schultz *Peanuts* cartoon, features Lucy in her typical position looking rather ruefully and reproachfully at Shroeder, who is ignoring her and playing the piano, and she tries to get his attention with this question: "Shroeder, do you know what love is?" And in the second panel is Shroeder standing at attention—"Um, love, a noun. A deep feeling, and intense desire for affiliation or attraction to another person or persons." In the third panel, he's back playing the piano again ignoring Lucy. She's staring off in the distance balefully saying, "On paper he's great."

In the second, a *Calvin and Hobbs* cartoon, Hobbs is saying, "I'm the decisive, take-charge type. I'm an actual leader. See, we'll go this way." And then Hobbs goes off, "Have fun." And then the last panel says, "The problem is that nobody wants to go where I want to lead them."

Exemplary leadership is the pathfinding capacity to create the social architecture or organizational design capable of inspiring people to follow, generating intellectual capital, and achieving competitive advantage.

TRICK #17

Release the Brainpower of Your People

In talking once to Percy Barnevik, the head of ABB and one of the most acclaimed executives in Europe, he said: "My major problem is this: How do I release the brainpower in the organization? That's the basis of intellectual capital."

Once when I visited Microsoft, I talked about intellectual capital, and they knew what I was talking about immediately. They said, "The only asset we have is human imagination."

The wellspring of innovation is intellectual capital—ideas, imagination, and insight. Look at the business press. An article in *Business Week* had as its cover "The Global Search for Brainpower." The *Wall Street Journal* ran a story on Jose Ignacio Lopez, a Basque Spaniard who once headed European operations for GM, who came to the states and did a marvelous job as purchasing officer. He was a real character, a charismatic leader. The same day he was to be introduced by Jack Smith, the head of GM, as the new head of GM's North American production, he and six GM colleagues ran off to Germany with 21 cartons of information. Lopez became head of Volkswagon's European operations. So what does GM do? They sue for $1 billion to get those 21 cartons of material back. Well, the case was settled out of court. They called it industrial espionage. What GM wanted was the brainpower of this man and his six colleagues.

How much of your intellectual capital is walking out the door with the people who leave your organization? And how much of your retained intellectual capital is well invested? What are your returns of that investment? Most leaders have no clue. But when you ask people how much of their brainpower they think they use on the job, the standard response is about 20 percent.

The individualism of today's workers makes the leader's job of releasing the brainpower of their people to benefit their organizations very challenging. I describe today's workplace as organized anarchy. This challenge is quite different from the one that faced 20th-century leaders. For them, it was much more of a linear world; organizations were hierarchical and bureaucratic. It was somewhat similar to the early notion of computing, in which you simply feed information into the system and it disgorges a solution. The mindset of control, order, and predict was fine in a stable environment, but in the 21st century, we will experience increasingly rapid change, and to deal with change, we will have to unhinge our organizations—they'll be confusing, chaotic places, full of surprises. Managers and leaders will be changed too, as they try to understand and to generate intellectual capital. They'll have to foster this creative collaboration within the organization and to translate the intention into reality.

As we enter the 21st century, I can't overestimate the significance of intellectual capital. No organization will remain in the phone book unless its leaders address the issue of how to generate intellectual capital.

In a 10-year study on work force quality study done by the University of Pennsylvania, they looked at 3,000 firms and discovered that a 10 percent increase in education leads to an 9 percent increase in productivity, and that a 10 percent increase in capital expenditures leads to a 3.5 percent increase in productivity.

We can find evidence of such increases in the best firms. Intel spends $4,000 a year per person for training and education. They have their own corporate college. Anderson Consulting spends 6 percent of their $10 billion revenue on education every year: 130 hours of education is required for every single Anderson professional. Motorola spends $200 million a year.

At General Electric, Jack Welch tells me that he spends about 4 percent of the payroll on education and training. Welch says: "My job is to listen, to search for, think of, spread ideas, to expose people, to get good ideas and role models. When self-confident people see a good idea, they love it." And Mark Fisher notes: "The true source of power in any corporation today is ideas. The rest is housekeeping. Ideas are the DNA of everything worthwhile."

Welch talks about GE as the idea pyramid. "We are obligated to be part of a constituency that's all pulling together to win, and there is no boundary, no hierarchy. It's a place for ideas. Ideas count. What you bring to the party counts, not this title, robes, and trappings. It's ideas. If I've got winning ideas, then I can get them from any place in the world, any corner. My job is to transmit them to the other corners. And so all these interactions are just building the idea pyramid. They're just shaping and learning. Everyday we're smarter. Every time I talk to people who know some aspect of management better than I do, I learn. They teach me more than I'll ever teach them."

The *New York Times* reported that General Motors, seeking to harness the knowledge of its employees worldwide, would appoint a senior-level chief learning officer to coordinate the spread of information on the company's vast holdings. GM appointed "Skip" LaFauve—the man who started the Saturn plant in Spring Hill, Tennessee, which transformed the way work is done at GM world-wide and brought about high employee involvement—as the new chief learning officer. Steve Kerr has the same job at GE. More organizations are appointing chief learning (or knowledge) officers to set up corporate universities. More companies are creating a role to spread good ideas fast inside the company.

Creating the social architecture to generate intellectual capital. I am convinced that the key to competitive advantage into the next century will be the capacity of leadership to create the social architecture that generates intellectual capital. Success will belong to those who unfetter greatness within their organizations and find ways to keep it there.

Others obviously think so, too, as evidenced by the increasing number of companies that build education into their programs. Some companies now spend at least 6 percent of their annual revenues on education and require every professional employee to take at least 100 hours of training each year. General Motors and others have named vice presidents for knowledge services. This institutionalization of education is not some fringe, feel-good benefit. It is tangible recognition that education gives the biggest bang for the corporate buck. Companies that invest more in education see a significant increase in productivity.

We've come about 50 percent of the way in terms of intellectual acceptance of participative management and employee involvement. Where we still need to go further is in the capacity of tough leadership to create a social architecture that will generate intellectual capital—ideas, innovations, learning, know-how. That's what it's all about.

The magnitude of the changes we face today makes it very difficult to think that we could ever get along without releasing the brainpower of people who work in teams and groups.

Again, the key to competitive advantage will be the capacity of top leadership to generate intellectual capital—to unleash know-how, imagination, creativity, initiative, and proactivity and then to use new and better ways to compensate people who excel. Knowing how to orchestrate different talents, knowing how to generate intellectual capital in groups and how to reward outstanding performance are the new keys to competitiveness.

Mortal Stakes. Given the confusion and the magnitude of complexity, we're playing for mortal stakes right now. Businesses will either change or die.

Leaders must start to deploy the brainpower of their people, individually and collectively. Most smart leaders are doing so. Those who take the position that "leaders are born and not made" often refuse to develop intellectual capital. They think that "you have to play the hand you're dealt." Yes, but there are many people, capable of leadership, who have never had a chance to deploy their talents or been encouraged to use their full capabilities on the job.

I don't blame today's leaders and organizations entirely for this misuse of brainpower. Followers, too, must share in the blame and be more proactive in their acquisition and application of work-related knowledge and skills. We all need to learn how to be led. I wish I had called my book *On Becoming a Leader* by a different title: *On Becoming a Follower.* I like the idea of "leaders of leaders" rather than "leaders of followers" because I believe that the capacities of effective leaders are very similar to the qualities of effective followers. What I expect from an effective follower is almost the same as what I expect from an effective leader. I think leaders are made great by their followers, and followers are made great by their leaders.

Leaders today must develop their social architecture so that it generates intellectual capital and encourages incredibly bright people, most of whom have big egos, to work together successfully and to deploy their own creativity. Most employees today are not just well-educated but also highly individualistic. The challenge is how to foster creative collaboration. To meet the challenge, leaders will have to reinvent themselves, redesign their leadership roles, and reinvent their organizations. Rather than just downsize, leaders must deploy the creativity of the workforce to recreate the company.

How do you deploy your workforce so that rather than downsizing, you can create new opportunities? One of my favorite leaders is Sidney Harman, who runs Harman International Industries, manufacturers of up-scale sound systems. He's increased productivity by about 30 percent, and he hasn't laid people off. He encourages his workforce to think about new possibilities, to create new inventions of their own core competencies. He's using all of his workforce to invent new jobs that will be productive and profitable. That is an example of what leaders must do: recreate their companies in ways that build intellectual capital.

I can't think of anything more significant than intellectual capital and release the brainpower, ideas, know-how, imagination, innovation in the workforce. This is what matters most. The frustrating thing is that intellectual capital is hard to measure. The *New York Times* once ran a rhapsodic front-page story about the IBM takeover of Lotus—a $3.5-billion acquisition. One paragraph in particular interested me: "Perhaps the most striking aspect of IBM's takeover bid, and the one that says the most about these times, is that it defies the accepted wisdom on the difficulties of trying to acquire a company whose primary value isn't in its machinery or real estate but rather in that most mercurial of assets—people." More graphically, Bill Gates said that the "only factory asset Microsoft has is human imagination." The best and brightest leaders know this. Disney's Michael Eisner, especially when he refers to the feature animation troupe, says that "my inventory goes home every night."

TRICK #18

Work for the Long-Term Interests of All Stakeholders

Today's leader has to take into account all of the stakeholders and not just the shareholders. The individual has to create a balance among these groups, despite the fact that, collectively, they may have conflicting objectives. Leaders must pay attention to the goals and purposes of the corporation and ask the question, "To whom is the business responsible?" Many executives might say the shareholders—and no one else. In fact, many corporations are run for the sole benefit of the shareholders. Everything they do is to increase shareholder value by driving up the price of the company's stock. But that overlooks other stakeholders, including employees, customers, and the community. The fact that institutional investors hold most of the stock in large corporations perpetuates this trend. And because these institutional investors are interested in increasing the wealth of their holdings—and they have the power to influence top management decisions in this direction—they have created a shift away from a stakeholder orientation to a shareholder mindset. This is why you see the emergence of executives who sharply downsize the company and then sell it and walk away with $100 million, and the shareholders also make out well. However, what about all the employees who lose their jobs as a result?

Have a long-term orientation. Leaders in every organization have a responsibility to employees, to suppliers, to customers, to the community—not only exclusively to the shareholders. I think wealth creation, while critical and a requirement, is not the only responsibility of leaders, not only the stakeholder in an organization. In an organization, there's the community, there's responsibility to employees, to the suppliers, to the customers, etc., not only exclusively to the shareholder.

I once participated in an international forum, chaired by Mikhail Gorbachev and attended by a lot of enlightened people like Ben Cohen of Ben and Jerry's, and Annita Roddick of The Body Shop. All of them are totally aware of the negative side of downsizing and trying to come up with a much more humane existence for organizations which is not just based on a Friedmanesque notion of one single goal of a corporation, which is to increase wealth of shareholders. It is a goal and an optimistic one. And I don't think it's because it's not just nice; it's necessary.

If you look at the work of Alice Tepper Marlin, who started the Council on Economic Priorities, and look at some measures of social and ethical concerns—what she shows very clearly is that year after year, those companies that have a stakeholder orientation, as opposed to a shareholder orientation, not only do well, they do good. So there seems to be a rough correlation between a socially conscious company with a moral compass and making stockholders happy.

There is a growing recognition of that. But there will always be the other side. We're not living in a utopia of socially conscious leaders.

THE TEMPORARY SOCIETY

As we continue to experience "temporary systems, nonpermanent relationships, turbulence, uprootedness, unconnectedness, mobility, and social upheaval," phrases like "embracing ambiguity," "identifying with the adaptive process," and "increasing our ability to collaborate" now appear as pallid, stale truths and, worse, mere platitudes and banalities.

I was reminded of this as I listened to an interview on National Public Radio of an editor of a hip, new business magazine, "Fast Company"—a "zine" as he called it, for knowledge workers of the new economy. The editor wondered if he was a little too sunshiny about the wonders of the information age, a little too upbeat about the staccato-like demands of the workplace. He was having second thoughts about deifying this big, bright, globally wired world.

I wonder, too, if my Brave New Leadership World, with all of its churning and transitions, adequately considered the psychological and economic dislocations and costs inherent in the temporary society. Joseph Schumpeter, the theoretical architect of modern capitalism, immortalized it with his famous metaphor, the "gale of creative destruction." Later on, he became melancholy about capitalism and its discontents.

I can hardly be considered melancholy today, but I don't think I took into account the shadowy side of change, the realization that every significant transition is a threat to one's self-esteem. Nor did I reckon with, let alone understand, the problems of the "underclass" in coping with social and personal changes. Just about everything I wrote was—had to be—refracted through the prism of my own experience.

For example, I didn't take into account the growing disparity between the nation's rich and its poor. Now, 1 percent of the population controls 40 percent of the wealth. An obscene offshoot of this is that the average CEO of a large company now earns 200 times more than the average worker, up from 40 percent in the 1970s. Nor did I fully take into account what the chronic state of change (and anxiety) would mean to the workforce, especially these days when nearly everyone (aside from Silicon Valley workers) worries about getting a pink slip. One paradox of our current prosperity is that with all of the affluence, the ordinary citizen feels less and less satisfied. Job satisfaction, financial satisfaction, and overall happiness are lower now than the average for the past 20 years. On top of that, all those competencies I once glorified such as "learning how to enter groups and leave them, " or "learning what roles are satisfying and how to attain them," or "learning how to develop intense and deep human relationships quickly—learn how to 'let go'" have become daily grist for Dilbert's cynical cartoons.

Seeing the future in the present is very like the science fiction of H. G. Wells's time machine. And this is possible only by the queer conjunction of simultaneous existence of societies at markedly different stages of economic, political, and social development coupled with the mass media, which transmit these images to all nations at any scale of development, from primitive villages to urban complexes. The advantage I speak of is the potential to seize the future through the examination and evaluation of the social and moral consequences of change before they invade—like a night train that suddenly appears, out of nowhere.

Whereas it is too late to slow down the pace of temporary societies, it is not too late (and it becomes necessary) to examine ways that may be more adaptive in coping with temporary systems, ways that could both realize our full human potentialities and extract whatever benefits modernization can bring.

To become authentic leaders who work hard for the long-term interests of all stakeholders and against the short-term interests of the temporary society, we must eternally confront and test our humanness and strive to become more fully human. The psychological consequences of temporary relationships are grave. We operate on a narrow range of the full spectrum of human potential, and for the most part, our organizational lives tend to compress the possibilities even more. Organization, by definition and certainly in practice, implies differentiation of function and specialization. Groups and interpersonal relationships tend to reinforce, if not worsen, this narrowness by calling on fewer and more stable and predictable functions. Essentially this is what the games-people-play is all about: a highly ritualized and complex habit that draws predictable responses from others so that one can play with ease, certainty, and without development. That's what make these games boring, like bad theater. These games can, of course, be rewarding and exhilarating, but most of the time they constrict their players to narrower and narrower lives, often compulsive and imprisoning.

To be more fully human means that we must work hard at coming to terms with unfamiliar aspects of our personalities, and we have to work equally hard to get other people to widen their responses so that they can understand and accept unfamiliarity and uncertainty. It also means that we must perceive our common humanness without fear of absorption or nothingness.

There are many forces conspiring against becoming fully human. Human relations and organizational life are both predicated on the assumption of shared and stable expectations. Most education shies away from or shuns these adaptive capacities, wishfully hoping that the student will possess them or that, like sex, he can find out about them from his buddies. So for the most part, we learn the significant things informally and badly, having to unlearn them later on in life when the consequences are frightfully expensive.

I would like to see educational programs in the art and science of being more fully human, which would take very seriously the kind of world we are living in, and help produce people who could not only cope with and understand this world but attempt to change it, We should help our students develop such interpersonal competencies as learning how to develop intense and deep human relationships—and how to "let go;" learning how to enter groups and leave them; learning what roles are satisfying and how to attain them; learning how to widen the repertory of feelings and roles available; learning how to cope more readily with ambiguity; learning how to develop a strategic comprehensibility of a new "culture" or system and what distinguishes it from other cultures; and learning how to develop a sense of one's uniqueness.

Somehow with all the mobility, chronic churning, and unconnectedness we envisage, it will become more important to develop some permanent or abiding commitment. It will be essential that we focus commitment on a person or an institution or an idea. This means that as general commitments become diffuse or modified, a greater fidelity to something or someone will be necessary to make us more fully human.

For some, the commitment may be derived from marriage. For others, a profession, work, church, or group may emerge as the source of fidelity. Ultimately, the world will require us to rely most heavily on our own resources. Hell, to paraphrase Sartre, may not be other people, but "the others" cannot always provide the sustenance and love that are so critical. We die alone, and to a certain extent we must live along, with a fidelity to ourselves. John Cage wrote a little "poem" that works as a proverb for our age: "We carry our homes within us, which enables us to fly."

TRICK #19

Adapt to a New Style of Leadership

Accepted theory and conventional wisdom concerning leadership have a lot in common. Both say that the success of a leader depends on the leader, the led, and the unique situation. How inadequate such formulations are when compared to the myths and primitive psychological issues surrounding such complexities as leadership and power. Leadership theory coexists with a powerful and parallel primitive reality. It is the latter reality, archetypal and mythic, that I have tried to upset by raising fears that our admirable ancestor and archetype—the aggressive, inner-directed autocrat—will become obsolete.

The phrase "the only constant is change" has reached the point of being a cliche, which at once anesthetizes us to its pain and stimulates grotesque fantasies about life in a brave new world with no place in the sun. Change is the "godhead" term for our age.

North America has become the only country to employ more people in services than in production of tangible goods. Today the growth industries, if we can call them that, are education, health, welfare, and other professional institutions. The problem facing organizations is no longer manufacturing—it is the management of large-scale, socio-technical systems.

There are other important obstacles and consequences of change. For example, the working population is younger, smarter, and more mobile. About half of America's population is under 25 years of age, about half go to college, and one out of every five families changes its address every year.

These changes compel us to look beyond bureaucracy for newer models of organizations that have the capability to cope with these conditions. The general direction of these changes—toward more service and professional organizations, toward more educated, younger, and mobile employees, toward more diverse, complex, science-based systems, toward a more turbulent and uncertain environment—forces us to consider new styles of leadership. Leading the enterprise of the future becomes a significant social process, requiring as much managerial as substantive competence. Leadership also depends on new forms of knowledge of skills not related to the primary task of the organization. The pivotal function in the leader's role has changed from a sole concern with the substantive to an emphasis on the interpersonal.

Challenges Facing Leaders

Let's review six challenges and examine the kinds of tasks and strategies linked to the solution of these problems.

1. Integration: Developing rewarding systems. To grasp the problem of integration, simply compute the ratio between what an individual gives and what he gets in his day-to-day transactions. Ask, Are the contributions to the organization about equivalent to the inducements received? Where there is high ratio between inducements and contribution, either the organization or the employee gets restless and searches for more rewarding environments or people.

What is interesting is that organizations frequently do not know what is truly rewarding. This is particularly true for the professional workers who will dominate the organizations of the future. With these employees, conventional policies and practices regarding incentives, never particularly sensitive, tend to be inapplicable.

Most organizations regard economic rewards as the primary incentive to peak performance. These are not unimportant to the professional, but—provided economic rewards are equitable—other incentives become far more potent. Avarice is not the spur of industry, particularly of professionals. Professionals tend to seek such rewards as full use of their talent and training: professional status (not necessarily within the organization); and opportunities for development and further learning. The main difference between the professional and hourly employee is that the former will not yield career authority to the organization.

The most important incentive, then, is to "make it" professionally, to be respected by professional colleagues. Loyalty to an organization may increase if it encourages professional growth. The "good place" to work resembles a super-graduate school, alive with dialogue and senior colleagues, where the employee will not only work to satisfy organizational demands, but perhaps primarily, those of his profession.

People today are looking toward work for self-realization, for personal growth that may not be task-related. Work, as we all must experience it, serves at least two psychic functions: that of binding us more closely to reality and of displacing libidinal components—narcissistic, aggressive, or even erotic—on to professional work and the human relations connected with it.

Many of the older forms of incentives, based on lower echelons of the need hierarchy (safety-economic-physiological), will have to be reconstituted. Even more profound will be the blurring of the boundaries between work and play, between affiliative and achievement drives.

2. Social Influence: Developing executive constellations. There are many issues involved in the distribution of power: psychological, practical, and moral. I will consider only the practical side. To begin with, it is quaint to think that one man or woman, no matter how omniscient and omnipotent, can comprehend, to say nothing of control, the diversity and complexity of the modern organization. Followers and leaders who think this is possible get entrapped in a false dream, a child's fantasy of absolute power and absolute dependence.

Today's administration must reflect the necessities imposed by size and complexity. In fact, there has been a general tendency in business to move away from a presidential form of power to a cabinet or team concept, with some exceptions where team management has been conceptualized and made explicit. There is still a long-standing masculine tendency to disparage such plural executive arrangements, but they are informally on the increase.

This executive constellation by no means implies an abdication of responsibility by the chief executive. It should reflect a functionally divided effort based on the distinct competencies of the constellation. It is a way of multiplying executive power through a realistic allocation of effort. Of course, this means also that top executives are chosen not only on the basis of their unique talents but on how complementary and compatible these skills and competencies are.

Despite all the problems inherent in executive constellations—problems of building an effective team, compatibility, and so forth—it is hard to see other valid solutions to the constraints of magnitude and sheer overload of the leader's role.

3. Collaboration: Building a collaborative climate. Related to the problem of developing an effective executive constellation is another key task of the leader—building a collaborative climate. An effective, collaborative climate is easier to experience and harder to achieve than a formal description, but most students of group behavior would agree that it should include the following ingredients: flexible and adaptive structure, utilization of member talents, clear and agreed-upon goals, norms of openness, trust, and cooperation, interdependence, high intrinsic rewards, and transactional controls, that is, members of the unit should have a high degree of autonomy and a high degree of participation in making key decisions.

Developing this group "synergy" is difficult, and most organizations take the easy way out: a "zero synergy" strategy. This means that the organization operates under the illusion that it will hire the best individuals in the world and then adopt a Voltairean stance of allowing them to "cultivate their own gardens." This strategy of isolation can best be observed in universities where it operates with great sophistication. Universities are, of course, a special case but until they take a serious look at their "anomic" existence, there is little hope that they will solve their vexing problems. Campus protests and riots are symptomatic of at least four self-contained social systems (students, faculty, administration, regents) without the trust, empathy, and interaction, to say nothing of tradition, to develop meaningful collaboration. To make matters worse, academics, by nature and reinforced by tradition, see themselves as loners and divergent. They want to be independent together, so to speak. Academic narcissism goes a long way on the lecture platform but may be positively dysfunctional for developing a community.

Another equally pernicious strategy is a "groupiness" where false harmony and conflict-avoidance persist. Synergy is hard to develop. Lack of experience and strong cultural biases against group efforts worsen the problem. Groups need time to develop. They require trust, interaction, communication, and commitment, and these ingredients require a period of gestation. I am continually amazed at expectation of easy maturity in groups of professionals.

Expensive and time consuming as it is, building synergetic and collaborative cultures has become essential. Modern problems are too complex and diversified for one person or one discipline. They require a blending of skills and perspectives, and only effective problem-solving units will be able to master them.

4. Adaptation: Identification with the adaptive process. Modern organizations, even more than individuals, are acutely vulnerable to the problem of responding flexibly and appropriately to new information. Symptoms of adaptive responses, at the extremes, are (1) a guarded, frozen, rigid response, denying the presence or avoiding the recognition of changes resulting most typically in organizational paralysis; or (2) susceptibility to change resulting in a spastic, unreliable faddism. There are times when openness to change is appropriate, and other times when it may be disastrous. Organizations, in fact, should reward people who act as counterchange agents, creating forces against the seduction of newness for its own sake.

How can leaders of these new organizations create an atmosphere of continuity and stability amid an environment of change? Whitehead put the problem well when he said: "The art of society consists first in the maintenance of the symbolic code, and secondly, in the fearlessness of revision. Those societies which cannot combine reverence to their symbols with freedom of revision must ultimately decay."

There is no easy solution to the tension between stability and change. We are not yet an emotionally adaptive society, though we are as close to having to become one as any society in history. Morison suggests that "we may find at least part of our salvation in identifying ourselves with the adaptive process and thus share some of the joy, exuberance, satisfaction, and security to meet changing times."

The remarkable aspect of our generation is its commitment to change in thought and action. Executive leadership must take responsibility in creating a climate that provides the security to identify with the adaptive process without fear of losing status and self-esteem. Creating an environment that would increase a tolerance for ambiguity and where one can make a virtue out of uncertainty, rather than one that induces hesitancy and its reckless counterpart, rather than one that induces hesitancy and its reckless counterpart, expediency, is one of the most challenging tasks for the new leadership.

5. Identity: Building supraorganizational goals and commitments. Organizations, like individuals, suffer from identity crises. They are not only afflictions that attack during adolescence, but chronic states pervading every phase of organizational development. The new organizations, coping within a turbulent environment, are particularly allergic to problems of identity. Professional and regional orientations lead frequently to fragmentation, intergroup conflicts, power plays, and rigid compartmentalization, devoid of any unifying sense of purpose or mission.

The university is a wondrous place for advanced battle techniques, for overshadowing its business counterparts in subterfuge and sabotage. Quite often a university becomes a loose collection of competing departments, schools, institutes, committees, centers, and programs, largely noncomunicating because of the multiplicity of specialist jargons and interests and held together, as Robert Hutchins once said, chiefly by a central heating system, or as Clark Kerr amended, by questions of what to do about the parking problem.

Such organizations are composed of people who love independence as fiercely as the ancient Greeks, but they resist what every Athenian, as a matter of course, gave time and effort for: "building and lifting up the common life." Certain individuals serve as articulating points between various groups and departments. Many individuals have a bicultural affinity with different languages and cultures. Organizations are composed of subcultures or "tribes," and such individuals play a vital role in keeping open the passages of communication.

All organizations need individuals who can provide articulation between seemingly inimical interests, who can transcend vested interests, regional ties, and professional biases. This is precisely what Mary Parker Follett had in mind when she discussed leadership in terms of an ability to bring about a "creative synthesis" between differing codes of conduct. Chester Barnard in his classic "Functions of the Executive" recognized this, as well as the personal energy and cost of political process. He wrote: "It seems to me that the struggle to maintain cooperation among men should as surely destroy some men morally as battle destroys some physically."

6. Revitalization: Controlling destiny. For the leader, revitalization means that the organization has to take a conscious responsibility for it sown evolution; that, without a planned methodology and explicit direction, the enterprise will not realize its full potential. For the leader, the issue of revitalization confronts him with the penultimate challenge: growth or decay.

The challenge for the leader is to develop a climate of inquiry and enough psychological and employment security for continual reassessment and renewal. The organizational culture must be developed which enables individuals to develop a willingness to participate in social revolution against unknown, uncertain, and implacable forces; and to develop a commitment to collect valid data and to act on limited information without fear of loss of control. The problem of revitalization is connected with the leader's ability to collect valid data, feed it back to the appropriate individuals, and develop action planning on the basis of data.

NEW CONCEPT OF LEADERSHIP

In addition to competence and comprehension of both social and technical systems, the new leader will have to possess interpersonal skills, not the least of which is the ability to defer his own immediate desires and gratifications to cultivate the talents of others. Here are some ways leaders can successfully cope with the new patterns.

1. Understand the social territory. "You gotta know the territory," sang "Professor" Harold Hill to his fellow salesmen in *The Music Man.* The "social territory" encompasses the complex and dynamic interaction of individuals, roles, groups, organizational and cultural systems. Organizations are, of course, legal, political, technical, and economic systems, but given our purposes we will focus primarily on the social system.

Leadership is as much a craft as science. The main instrument or tool for the leader-as-craftsman is himself, and how creatively he can use his own personality. This is particularly important for leaders to understand, for they, like physicians, are "iatrogenic," that is, physicians are capable of spreading as well as curing disease. And again, like the physician, it is important for the leader to follow the maxim "know thyself" so that he can control some of the pernicious effects he may create unwittingly. Unless the leader understands his actions and effects on others, he may be a carrier rather than a solver of problems. The leader must be willing and able to set up reliable mechanisms of feedback so that he can not only conceptualize the social territory of which he is an important part, but realize how he influences it.

2. Use an action-reflection model of leadership. This model of leadership involves (1) the collection of data, (2) feedback to appropriate sources, and (3) action planning. The "hangup" in most organizations is that people tend to distort and suppress data (particularly in communicating to higher levels) for fear of retaliation or on the basis of other fantasized or real threats. Samuel Goldwyn once called his top staff together after a particularly bad box-office flop and said, "Look, you guys, I want you to tell me exactly what's wrong with this operation and my leadership—even if it means losing your job!"

3. Embrace the concept of system-intervention. Research has shown that productivity can be modified by group norms, that training effects fade out and deteriorate if the training effects are not compatible with the goals of the social system, that group cohesiveness is a powerful motivator, that intergroup conflict is a major problem, that individuals take many of their cues and derive a good deal of their satisfaction from their primary work groups, and that identification with the small work group turns out to be the y stable predictor of productivity.

The fact that this evidence is so often cited and so rarely acted upon leads me to infer that there is something naturally preferable in locating the sources of problems in the individual and diagnosing situations as functions of faulty individuals rather than as symptoms of malfunctioning social systems. Pinning the blame or credit on individuals is much easier than identifying system problems, which are, by definition, more complex and abstract. It is simply easier to talk about people than abstractions.

Individuals, living amid complex and subtle organizational conditions, do tend to oversimplify and distort complex realities so that people rather than conditions embody the problem. This tendency can be seen when members of organizations take on familial nicknames, such as "Dad," "Big Brother," "Mom," "Mother Hen," "Dutch Uncle," and so on. We can see it in distorted polarization such as the "good guy" leader and his "hatchet man" assistant. These grotesques seem to bear such little resemblance to the actual people that one has to ask what psychological needs are being served by this complex process of denial and stereotyping.

An organization absorbs an enormous amount of feeling that is projected onto it by its membership. The primitive drama of dreams and childhood can be parlayed into a form of "aesopianism" where individuals, at some distance from the citadels of power, can analyze, distort, stereotype, project, and sublimate all their own deeper wished and fears into the shadowy reaches of the organization. If there weren't kings and queens, we would have to invent them as therapeutic devices to allay anxieties about less romantic, more immediate mothers and fathers, brothers and sisters.

Organizations are big, complex, wondrous, and hamstrung with inertia. Impotence and alienation imprison the best of people, the most glorious of intentions. There is a myth that the higher one goes up the ladder, the more freedom and potency one experiences. In fact, this is frequently not the case, as almost any chief executive will report. Paradoxically, the higher one goes, the more tethered and bound he or she feels by expectations and commitments. In any case, as one gets entrapped by inertial and impotence, it is easier to blame heroes and villains than the system. For if the problems are embroidered into the fabric of the social system, complex as they are, the system can be changed. The effect of locating problems in people rather than systems frequently leads to organizational paralysis because changing human nature often appears to be and frequently is more difficult than changing systems.

Other Directed Leadership

Today we are more "other-directed" than our parents or grandparents—who would have been characterized as "inner-directed." These character types refer essentially to the ways we are influenced and the forces that shape our perspectives. Other-directed people takes their cues from their peer group rather than from their parents. They take their relationships more seriously than they do their relatives. Their ideology, values, and norms are transmitted to them and accepted by the particular social group that they associate with. They are "pleasers," cooperative and accommodating. Inner-directed people, to extend the exaggeration, responds to some internal gyroscope, typically internalized parental pressures. They respond not to any social grouping but to some inner cues. Inner-directed people are rigid, unyielding, and act on principles.

The type of organization undoubtedly influences the style of leadership behavior rewarded. Some organizations tend to reward the aggressive, forceful, decisive, inner-directed leader; others reward the cooperative, adaptable, other-directed leader. In the "growth industries" of education, health, welfare, government, and professional organizations, the prime requisites of a leader will be interpersonal competence and other-directedness.

This new concept of leadership constitutes an active method for producing conditions where people and ideas and resources can be cultivated to optimum effectiveness and growth.

The most appropriate metaphor I have found to characterize adaptive leadership is an "agricultural" model. The leader's job, is to build a climate where growth and development are culturally induced. Until recent times, the metaphor most commonly used to describe power and leadership in organization derived from Helmholtz's laws of mechanics. Max Weber, who first conceptualized the model of bureaucracy, wrote: "Bureaucracy is like a modern judge who is a vending machine into which the pleadings are inserted along with the fee and which then disgorges the judgment with its reasons mechanically derived from the code." The vocabulary for adaptive organizations requires an organic metaphor, a description of a process, not structural arrangements. This process must include such terms as open, dynamic systems, developmental, organic, and adaptive.

The key aspect is the ability of the leader to develop collaborative relationships. This is not to say that the leader should be a "good guy" or seek popularity, but it does mean that he will have to learn to negotiate and collaborate. The leader can't know everything, and his colleagues have the information and competencies that he or she needs. How the leader gets access to and uses information depends entirely on his or her ability to collaborate with others. Power accrues to those who can gather and control information wisely.

The psychological "contract" between leader and led is more satisfying and almost always more productive if the relationship is more egalitarian. This is particularly true with professionals and a young, intelligent workforce with a "participating democracy" ideology. The most productive professionals work in situations where the processes of determining work objectives are transactional rather than unilateral, Transactional arrangements occur when leaders and followers reach decisions together—collaboratively. When standards and objectives are imposed by leaders, followers perform poorly. One of the most difficult aspect of this style of leadership is to confront those recalcitrant parts of the system that are retarded, stunted, or afraid to grow. This will require enormous energy, saintly patience, and a sophisticated optimism in growth (or a high tolerance for disenchantment).

This new concept of leadership relies less on the leader's knowledge about a particular topic than it does on the understanding and possession of four competencies: (1) knowledge of large, complex human systems, (2) practical theories of guiding these systems, theories that encompass methods for the seeding, nurturing, and integrating individuals and groups, (3) interpersonal competence, particularly the sensitivity to understand the effects of one's own behavior on others and how one's own personality shapes one's particular leadership style and value system, and (4) a set of values and competencies that enables one to know when to confront and attack, if necessary, and when to support and provide the safety so necessary for growth.

I'm amused to note that this view of leadership is often construed as "passive" or "weak" or "soft" or more popularly, "permissive" and dismissed with a patronizing shrug. But I deem this role of leadership to be clearly more demanding and formidable than any other precedent, from king to pope. Construing this new leadership role in such passive and insipid terms may betray some anxiety aroused by the eclipse of a distant, stern, and strict father. That may be the only kind of authority we have experienced firsthand and know intimately. Yet, as this new person of power—other-directed and interpersonally competent—emerges, then not only new myths and archetypes will have to be created to substitute for the old, familial ones but new ways will have to be developed to dramatize the advent of new heroes.

TRICK #20

Form New Global Alliances

Jan Carlzon, CEO of Scandinavian Air System (SAS), illustrates one element that will distinguish the vision of 21st-century leaders from the current model. His is a global vision; he is fully aware of the need for transnational networking and alliances.

Carlzon is not alone. A recent United Research Co./Harris survey of 150 CEOs of Forbes 500 companies found that they saw the greatest opportunity and challenge for the future in the global market. In the same vein, senior-level managers polled in a Carnegie-Mellon University survey of business school alumni named competing effectively on a global basis as the most difficult management issue for the next decade.

SIX PIVOTAL FORCES

I see six pivotal forces working on the world today, and leadership is necessary for coping with each of these forces: (1) global interdependence, (2) technology, (3) mergers and acquisitions, (4) deregulation and re-regulation, (5) demographics and values, and (6) environment.

One of the first things the astute business person checks daily now is the yen-dollar ratio: 50 percent of downtown Los Angeles is owned by the Japanese, and so is a large hunk of the popular Riviera Country Club. Foreign investment in America—in real estate, finance, and business—continues to escalate. But the changes aren't simply on our shores. In 1992, when Europe becomes truly a Common Market, it will contain 330 million consumers, as compared with 240 million in this country.

American leaders who want to be a part of that new market are planning now. Michael Eisner of Disney has sent Robert Fitzpatrick to France to head up the new EuroDisney project. CalFed, which already has a bank in England, is preparing for the future with plans for banks in Brussels, Barcelona, Paris, and Vienna. In Spain, AT&T has spent $220 million for a semiconductor plant, and General Electric has budgeted $1.7 billion for a plastics facility. Ford, Nissan, Sony, and Matsushita have opened factories in or near Barcelona.

In most cases, however, buying into Europe is prohibitively expensive. The shrewd leaders of the future are recognizing the wisdom of creating alliances with other organizations whose fates are correlated with their own. The Norwegian counterpart of Federal Express—which has 3,500 employees, one of the largest companies in Norway—is setting up a partnership with Federal Express. First Boston has linked up with Credit Suisse, forming FBCS. GE has set up a number of joint ventures with GE of Great Britain, meshing four product divisions. Despite the names, the companies hadn't been related. GE had considered buying its British namesake, but ultimately chose alliance rather than acquisition.

Buying in is not the choice of the Europeans themselves: Glaxco, a British pharmaceutical firm, made a deal with Hoffman-LaRoche for the distribution of Zantac, a stomach tranquilizer, and knocked SmithKline Beecham's Tagamet out of the game. Kabi Virtum, a Swedish pharmaceutical company, is looking for a partner in Japan to build a joint laboratory, in exchange for which the Japanese would get help in licensing drugs in Sweden.

And getting back to Jan Carlzon—he tried to buy Sabena, and when he couldn't, he established an alliance with the rival airline. SAS also works with an Argentine airline and with Eastern Airlines, sharing gates and connecting routes. The global strategy is firmly rooted in Carlzon's vision for the SAS.

All leaders' guiding visions provide clearly marked road maps for their organizations, so that every member can see in which direction the corporation is going. The communication of the vision generates excitement about the trip. The plans for the journey create order out of chaos, instill confidence and trust, and offer criteria for success. The group knows when it has arrived.

LEADER AS TRANSFORMER

Around the globe, we face three threats: the threat of annihilation as a result of nuclear accident or war, the threat of a worldwide plague or ecological catastrophe, and a deepening leadership crisis. In my mind, the leadership crisis is the most urgent and dangerous of the threats we face today, if only because it is insufficiently recognized and little understood.

Signs of the crisis are alarming and pervasive. Witness the change in leadership at some of our most respected corporations. In politics, no head of a developed, democratic nation has more than a tentative hold on his or her constituency. In one country, the party in office has the support of only 3 percent of the population. Twice as many people—6 percent—believe Elvis is still alive.

The leadership crisis appears to be spreading. In the United States, senators are resigning, some without encouragement of scandal. The mood of the populace is unsettled, angry, sometimes foul, even murderous. And those who ostensibly lead agree only that things are terrible and getting worse.

Among the general population, cynicism is rampant. I don't recall such a widespread loss of faith in our major institutions even during the tumultuous 1960s. Indeed, I can't remember a time when so many of our leaders themselves were so vocally disenchanted with government as they are today.

The world seems to have been transformed virtually overnight and appears ripe to change again by tomorrow morning. Inevitably, such global change has corporate repercussions.

Today CEOs are forced to deal not only with the exigencies of their own organizations, but also with a new social reality. These leaders face increasing and unfamiliar sources of competition as a result of global markets, capital, labor, and information technology. Future organizations will be networks, clusters, cross-functional teams, temporary systems, ad hoc task forces, lattices, modules, matrices—almost anything but pyramids. The configurations that succeed will be less hierarchical and have more linkages based on common goals rather than on traditional reporting relationships.

To be successful, organizations must have flexible structures that enable them to be highly responsive and adaptive. They must be leaner, have fewer layers, and engage in transformational and nontraditional alliances and mergers. And they must understand a global array of business practices, customers, and cultures.

TRICK #21

Reinvent Your Organization

Reengineering is reinventing the enterprise by challenging its existing doctrines, practices, and activities and then innovatively redeploying its capital and human resources into cross-functional processes. This reinvention is intended to optimize the organizations competitive position, its value to shareholders, and its contribution to society.

Reinventing the enterprise means permanently transforming its orientation and direction. It means challenging traditional values, historical precedents, tried-and-true processes, and conventional wisdom and replacing them with entirely different concepts and practices. It means redirecting and retraining people.

The very cultural fiber must be interrogated and redefined. Work flows must be examined and redesigned. Technology must be redirected to enable new cross-functional processes and a flatter structure. New systems must be created. Ways of measuring and rewarding performance and success must be rethought.

FIVE ELEMENTS

Reengineering has five essential elements: a bold vision, a systematic approach, a clear intent and mandate, a specific methodology, and effective and visible leadership. If any one of these elements is missing, the change effort is not reengineering.

1. A bold vision. The start is a bold vision, and the passion to turn that vision into reality. The vision and passion may change an entire industry. Disney, for example, set out to regain dominance by reinventing its entertainment operations. Home Depot reengineered the way people shop for their home-remodeling materials when it launched the concept of retail warehousing with huge quantities of in-stock items, everyday low prices, and highly paid and knowledgeable workers. In doing so, it not only reengineered the traditional building-supply industries, but also created a completely new retailing concept.

2. A systemic approach. Reengineering is systemic, not situational. It has far-reaching, organization-wide implications and is not restricted to just one issue, procedure, task, activity, function, or unit. The process of customer service, for example, spans the entire organization. Reengineering arranges all activities associated with customer service which were previously divided into separate units, into processes that have a continual flow, accelerated velocity, a consolidated function, and a common system of management practices and performance measurements. This restructuring leads to uniformity in dealing with customers and greatly increases the probability that customers will see the results.

3. A clear intent and mandate. Few organizations embark on reengineering with a clear intent and mandate. Often, executives engage in some change effort and after the fact refer to that effort as "reengineering." To effect systemic, lasting change, executives must start with that specific intention and must realize that the end point will be an entirely different enterprise. Creating a new enterprise requires the ongoing support of top management; there's no other way to ensure that the necessary resources are applied to plan, manage, implement, and sustain the reengineering effort.

4. A specific methodology. Unlike the accounting and legal professions, reengineering has no codified rules, educational requirements, or professional standards. As reengineering is still evolving there is very little information on how to perform the process. In particular, there's an absence of useful how-to material. A specific methodology is critical. Both the leader of the reengineering process and the employees who implement it need to know exactly what is to be done every step of the way. In the absence of specific techniques, the reengineering process can result in chaos and lasting scars.

5. Effective and visible leadership. Reengineering and the systemic transformation that results require effective and visible leadership. The leader of the process must have several skills and abilities, among them: creativity, visionary influence, solid knowledge of the business, credibility (achieved through a track record of successful experience in reengineering), impeccable character, excellent judgment, and exceptional people skills, including the abilities to select the right people for implementing the reengineering effort and to provide positive coaching for them. If the leader does not have these skills, the reengineering effort will be compromised.

FIVE GOALS

Reengineering has five goals:

1. Increase productivity. Reengineering seeks to increase productivity by creating innovative and seamless processes that have an uninterrupted flow and occur in a natural order, with a natural velocity. The paradigm of vertial "silos" of tasks and responsibilities is replaced with a cross-functional, flatter, networked structure. The classical, top-down approach to control and decision making is replaced with an approach organized around core processes, characterized by empowerment, and closer to the customer. Traditional boundaries (which create gaps and "pass-offs" in work and diminish the value, speed, and quality of processes) are eliminated.

2. Optimize value to shareholders. Reengineering produces benefits for shareholders in five areas: (1) increased employee interest in and appreciation of the enterprise, its leadership, its products or services, and its customers; (2) improved internal cooperation, communication, teamwork, and understanding of needs; (3) increased employee knowledge of the organization's direction, its role in the marketplace, its competitors, and its identity; (4) improved matching of employee skills and empowerment to responsibilities and processes; (5) new individual- and group-performance measures that are closely aligned with the marketplace, the value of the work performed, and the contribution made. Employees who are involved with reengineering develop a profound sense of ownership that helps the organization achieve long-term growth and competitiveness.

3. Achieve quantum results. Our experience indicates the potential for these results: productivity improvements of 25 to 100 percent; head-count redeployments of 25 to 50 percent; inventory reductions of 40 to 50 percent; cycle-time improvements of 50 to 300 percent; indirect-cost improvements of 25 to 50 percent. These are not the traditional 5 to 15 percent incremental gains that most organizations have been content to achieve.

4. Consolidate functions. Reengineering seeks to create a leaner, flatter, and faster organization. The ability to rapidly assimilate innovations, market needs, technological developments, customer trends, and competitor initiatives is a trademark of reinvented times.

5. Eliminate unnecessary levels and work. Reengineering constructively challenges the organization's hierarchy and activities in terms of their value, purpose, and content. Activities that represent little value to shareholders or contribute little to competitiveness are either restructured or eliminated. Reinvention requires the continual assessment of the organization, its management practices, its people, its systems, its customers, and its environment. Ask five questions repeatedly: (1) Why do we do the things we do in the way we do them? (2) What value is produced for customers and shareholders by performing this activity in this way? (3) How could we perform this activity in a different way to enhance value? (4) What innovative or breakthrough results do we want to achieve? (5) What talents are required, and who has them?

Reengineering transforms an organization from what it is now into an unlimited universe of what it could be. Reengineering is not a fad; it is a distinct and permanent change in how an organization can be led, managed, and operated.

TRICK 22

Solve Problems Before
They Have Names

Systems and structures stay viable only by continually transforming themselves to meet the demands of changing climates. Change continues to be the one given of our time—dizzying, unpredictable, relentless change that cries for temporary systems that can be dismantled as soon as they become outmoded. If you have the unenviable task of keeping the map of your world up to date, you are likely one harried cartographer, wishing you were working on an Etch-a-Sketch.

The leaders who thrive and the organizations that succeed today embrace change instead of resisting it. Those who struggle are too slow, too weighed down with their own agendas and priorities to compete. Certain organizations are doomed because they simply do not work, or, more precisely, work fast enough. Today's most viable institutions are dancers, not marchers. They see opportunities, exploit them, and then move nimbly onto the next challenge, while slow organizations are gearing up to study the problem at hand. Success goes to those who can identify and solve problems almost before they have names.

Prediction is a democratic pastime. In authoritarian societies there is little call for it—life is static, change is slow, innovation is highly controlled, and, on the rare occasion when it occurs, change is announced from above. The wild guesses about the future so popular in our society are meaningless when "the future'—what little there is of it—is funneled through the tiny orifice of centralized authority, which disapproves of attempts to anticipate its leaden decisions.

A democratic society is a complex, confusing, erratic, and continually evolving organism that grows in all directions at once. Making one's way in it calls for an extraordinary degree of alertness, sensitivity, and flexibility. Predictions are made and altered daily as the evolutionary winds shift. Authoritarians are not happy with this spinning weather vane we take for granted. They want an iron rooster that points every day in exactly the same direction. They don't want predictions; they want predictability. They want to control the uncontrollable, which is why they are so obsessed with disciplining the most spontaneous products of nature: children, animals, and all growing things.

In the past this obsession with control had support from science, with its constant search for "predictability," that is, the certainty that would render "predictions"—guessing the future—unnecessary. But with the advent of the Uncertainty Principle and Chaos Theory, science has now irrevocably committed itself to the democratic camp, to the realization that life, nature, the world around us, all have an agenda—and we are a part of it, not the master of it, and must meet it on its own terms. Democracy is not about control. It is about attunement.

Most of us grew up in bureaucratic organizations that were dominated by a command-and-control orientation. This bureaucratic machine model, designed to harness manpower and resources, is characterized by strong divisions of labor, narrow specialization, and hierarchies, with lots of levels. Most organizations today still have that kind of command-and-control, macho mentality. But the organizations of the future will resemble networks or modules. The successful ones will have flattened hierarchies and more cross-functional linkages.

FROM MONOLITH TO LEGO SET

No longer a monolith, the successful modern corporation is like a Lego set whose parts can be regularly reconfigured as circumstances change. The old paradigm that exalted control, order, and predictability is giving away to a nonhierarchical order in which all employees' contributions are solicited and acknowl-edged and in which creativity is valued over blind loyalty. Sheer self-interest motivates the change. Organizations that encourage broad participation, even dissent, make better decisions.

Adaptability has become the most important determinant of an organization's survival, and information drives the organiza-tion of the future. The person who has information wields more power than ever before. Those who are not over-committed to the status quo are in the best position to take advantage of change and innovation, and this certainly applies to women, who have been excluded from the authoritarian hierarchical struc-tures. As men were squeezed by authoritarian culture into the emotional corset of macho competitiveness, it fell to women to take care of all other human needs—emotional expression, rela-tionships, cooperation, nurturance, and so on. They were forced to become skilled at diplomacy, mediation, negotiation, compro-mise, recognition of the needs and rights of others. But these are precisely the skills that are needed in a democracy. Men who practice democracy tend still to be caught up in the belligerent assumptions of the authoritarian past: they talk constantly of "standing up to" and "not being swayed by" and "not giving into" and being "firm" or "tough,"as if rigidity were a virtue and problem solving a form of hand-to-hand combat.

Men have committed themselves to an individualistic, linear, competitive, atomistic, and mechanistic conceptual world—one which they now dominate. But ironically, science—once the most extreme expression of this world—has now rendered it obsolete.

In the past, men disparaged this way of looking at the world as "magical thinking," typical of women, children, and the inhab-itants of nonliterate societies. But now it has become the accept-ed conceptual framework. Nature, it seems, is relentlessly nonlinear, and those who fail to recognize this simple truth are destined to be left behind, mired in an antiquated mind-set.

Women are better adapted to the confusion and chaos that chronic change, democracy, and the new sciences together pro-duce. Their control needs, on average, tend to be less exaggerated than those of men, who like to dominate their environment and make it simple and predictable. Women are more comfortable with the chaos that small children generate and are better able to cope with several different processes at the same time. Housewives who try to cook, clean, and shop while noisy children race everywhere receive optimum training for democratic living.

Some will object, of course, that women who become corporate managers do not necessarily exhibit these traits but are often more controlling, rigid, competitive, and authoritarian than men. This will be true as long as women are a small minority in a "man's world," having to prove they have traits they are not expected to have—having to show they are "tough" enough to do the job. In the same way, blacks who have succeeded in the same situation have often had to be "whiter" than whites—more conservative, uptight, restrained, and so forth. Once a group ceases to be a rarity, this need to over-conform to tradition eases.

Some form of participatory management is common in companies engaged in invention. Companies on the cutting edge of technological change tend to be forced by their very nature to operate by democratic principles, and those that become bureaucratized and hierarchical usually find themselves upstaged by egalitarian newcomers.

Transitions are difficult. The gradual global shift from authoritarianism to democracy—from war to peace, from machismo to cooperation, from domination to attunement, from linear science to nonlinear science—is a paradigm shift of unprecedented magnitude. Such a change inevitably causes great strain and confusion for us poor human beings hungry for stability and familiarity. We reach excitedly toward the future with one hand and cling desperately to our old concepts with the other. Is it any wonder we feel pulled apart at times? We can see this strain in the so-called lack of civility in our daily lives today, in the frustration that produces so much ranting on the airwaves and so often leads to violence. We see our ambivalence in our high tech sci-fi fantasies that begin with so much sophistication but usually end in some form of hand-to-hand combat. We see it again in our many movies about brutal post-apocalyptic words— worlds created by the disastrous macho values we now embrace, yet at the same time rendering those same values once again meaningful and desirable.

Reality is less dramatic. Change is a gradual, two-steps-forward-one-back process, but we may reasonably expect to muddle through. There will be plenty of disasters and atrocities along the way for change never comes cheaply. Nobody likes becoming obsolete, and those who hold advantages seldom give them up without a struggle. But the process cannot be stopped without a global catastrophe; it gathers momentum every day. It will never be easy for us, but it may help a little to recognize what's happening and to admit that it all makes us a little uncomfortable, whether we thing we welcome change or fight it tooth and nail.

Cynics point out that business leaders who extol the virtues of democracy on ceremonial occasions would be the last to think of applying them in their own organizations. To the extent that this is true, however, it reflects a state of mind that by no means is peculiar to businessmen but that characterizes all Americans—perhaps all citizens of democracies.

This attitude, briefly, is that democracy is a nice way of life for nice people, despite its manifold inconveniences—a kind of expensive and inefficient luxury, like owning a large medieval castle. Feelings about it are for the most part affectionate, even respectful, but a little impatient. There are probably few men of affairs in America who have not at some time nourished in their hearts the blasphemous thought that life would go much more smoothly if democracy could be relegated to some kind of Sunday morning devotion.

The bluff practicality of the "nice-but-inefficient" stereotype masks a hidden idealism, however, for it implies that institutions can survive in a competitive environment through the sheer good-heartedness of those who maintain them. We would like to challenge this notion and suggest that even if all of those benign sentiments were eradicated today, we would awaken tomorrow to find democracy still firmly entrenched, buttressed by a set of economic, social, and political forces as practical as they are uncontrollable.

Democracy has been so widely embraced, not because of some vague yearning for human rights but because under certain conditions it is a more "efficient" form of social organization. Those nations of the world that have endured longest under conditions of relative wealth and stability are democratic, whereas authoritarian regimes have, with few exceptions, either crumbled or maintained a precarious and backward existence. It seems that democracy is the only system that can successfully cope with the changing demands of contemporary civilization.

There are signs that our business community is becoming aware of this law. Several of the most rapidly blooming companies in the United States boast unusually democratic organizations. Even some large, established corporations have moved steadily toward democratization. Frequently they begin by feeling that administrative vitality and creativity are lacking in the older systems. So, they enlist the help of outside consultants and trainers. Executives and even entire management staffs have been sent to participate in training programs to learn skills and attitudes that just 20 years ago would have been denounced as anarchic and revolutionary. At these meetings, status prerogatives and traditional concepts of authority are severely challenged.

What we have in mind when we use the term democracy is not permissiveness or laissez-faire but a system of values—a climate of beliefs governing behavior—that people are internally compelled to affirm by deeds as well as words. These values include: (1) full and free communication, regardless of rank and power; (2) a reliance on consensus, rather than the more customary forms of coercion or compromise to manage conflict; (3) the idea that influence is based on technical competence and knowledge rather than on the vagaries of personal whims or prerogatives of power; (4) an atmosphere that permits and even encourages emotional expression as well as task-oriented acts; and (5) a human bias, one that accepts the inevitability of conflict between the organization and the individual but that is willing to cope with and mediate this conflict on rational grounds

Democracy becomes a functional necessity whenever a social system is competing for survival under conditions of chronic change. The most familiar variety of such change is technological innovation. Because change has now become a permanent and accelerating factor, adaptability to change becomes increasingly the most important single determinant of survival. The profit, the saving, the efficiency, the morale of the moment becomes secondary to keeping the door open for rapid readjustment to changing conditions.

The Greeks cautioned against calling a man happy before he had achieved a peaceful death; we would caution against calling any organization efficient until it has met at least one new and unexpected threat to its existence.

The passing of years has also given the coup de grace to another force that retarded democratization—the Great Man who with brilliance and farsightedness could preside with dictatorial powers at the head of a growing organization and keep it at the vanguard of American business. In the past he was usually a man with a single idea, or a constellation of related ideas, which he developed brilliantly. This is no longer enough (and the Great Man may, in fact, be a Great Woman).

Today, just as the head of an organization begins to reap the harvest of his imagination, he finds that someone else has suddenly carried the innovation a step further, or has found an entirely new and superior approach to it, and he is suddenly outmoded. How easily can he abandon his idea, which contains all his hopes, his ambitions, his very heart? His aggressiveness now begins to be a liability, a dead hand, an iron shackle upon the flexibility and growth of the company. But he cannot be removed. In the short run, the firm would even be hurt by his loss, since its prestige derives to such an extent from his reputation. And by the time he has left, the organization will have receded into a secondary position within the industry. It may even decay further when his personal touch is lost. The cult of personality still exists, of course, but it is rapidly fading. More and more large corporations predicate their growth not on heroes but on solid management teams.

What is confusing to me is the tendency to equate conformity with autocracy, to see the new industrial organization as one in which all individualism is lost except for a few villainous individualistic manipulators at the top. But this is absurd in the long run. The trend toward the organization man is also a trend toward a looser and more flexible organization in which roles are to some extent interchangeable and no one is dispensable. To many people this trend is a monstrous nightmare, but one should at least not confuse it with the nightmares of the past. It may mean anonymity and homogeneity, but it does not and cannot mean authoritarianism, in the long run, despite the bizarre anomalies and hybrids that may arise in a period of transition.

The reason it cannot is that it arises out of a need for flexibility and adaptability and the need to maximize the availability of appropriate knowledge, skill, and insight under conditions of great variability.

While the "organization man" has titillated our imaginations, the concept has masked a far more fundamental change now taking place—the rise of professional specialists, holding advanced degrees in such abstruse sciences as cryogenics or computer logic, and in business disciplines. These people seemingly derive their rewards from inward standards of excellence, from their professional societies, from the intrinsic satisfaction of their standards, and not from their bosses. Because they have degrees, they travel. They are not good company men; they are uncommitted except to the challenging environments where they can "play with problems."

These new professionals are remarkably compatible with democratic systems. For, like these new men, democracy seeks no new stability, no end point; it is purposeless, save that it purports to ensure perpetual transition, constant alteration, ceaseless instability. It attempts to upset nothing but only to facilitate the potential upset of anything. Democracy and our new professionals identify primarily with the adaptive process, not the establishment.

Like children, they are naturally imaginative, and this is another reason why they are so essential. They can envision things being different from the way they are—a vision often lost by managers who are ground down by everyday "realities."

I like to think of myself as an eternal optimist. Although the pool may be diminishing, there are still plenty of young people out there with vivid imaginations and the artistic ability to produce superior creative material. Prophets of doom have had a low success rate over the years, usually by underestimating human resiliency. However much we "herd" our children and creative "cats" and "dogs" around, from one program, meeting or activity to another, they still manage to find islands of independence, and no doubt always will.

TRICK #23

Be a Leader of Leaders

We are undergoing a period of "creative destruction." And what this means for leaders is that they will have to keep recomposing and reinventing their leadership—in effect, becoming a leader of leaders. Because of the rapid changes, not only the CEOs but all leaders at every level need to reinvent themselves and redesign their leadership roles. Leaders must also constantly reinvent the organization. Rather than just downsizing, leaders need to deploy the creativity of the workforce to recreate the company.

The leader of the new organization has to be a leader of leaders. This is where you need true leadership, leadership that continues to provide the necessary balance. This calls for a new kind of leader. Leaders of federations don't think of their associates as "troops." And the associates don't think of their leaders as generals.

You can't be the only one making decisions. You can't be the only leader. Rather, you have to create an environment in which other leaders, who subscribe to your vision, can make effective decisions—an environment in which people at all levels are empowered to be leaders.

The leader of today has to have faith in the power of people to solve their problems locally. He or she is responsible for establishing the"why" and the "what—the overarching vision and purpose—but the rest of the leaders are responsible for the "how."

A central task for the leader of leaders is the development of other leaders. That means creating conditions that enhance the ability of all employees to make decisions and create change. The leader must actively help his or her followers to reach their full leadership potential.

As Max De Pree, the chairman and CEO of Herman Miller, once put it: "The signs of outstanding leadership appear primarily among the followers. Are they reaching their potential? Are they learning?"

So tomorrow's leaders will spend much time nurturing other leaders. To prepare for the challenges of tomorrow, leaders today must enroll people in an exciting, insanely significant vision. Leaders have to realize that people would much rather live lives dedicated to an idea or a cause that they believe in, than lead lives of aimless diversion. Effective leaders are all about creative collaboration, about creating a shared sense of purpose, because people need meaningful purpose. That's why we live. The power of an organization will be that shared sense of purpose. With a shared purpose you can achieve anything.

CREATING LEADERS

Leaders are made, not born. There is no genetic marker for leadership. Basically, leadership is learned on the job.

In our studies at the University of Southern California, we asked leaders how they learned to be leaders. They point to challenges they faced and overcame, learning through mistakes and going forward. None say they learned leadership by taking academic courses or by getting an MBA or Ph.D. They learned it mostly from their bosses—good and bad ones.

Why don't organizations do a better job of creating leaders? Part of the answer is that leaders challenge the system; they question the gospel. Most organizations in times of change don't reward that behavior; they reward people who follow. George Bernard Shaw said: "All great progress is made by unreasonable men who make the world adapt to them."

We're moving to a stage of idea-intensive production and away from material-intensive production. Leaders realize that if they're going to be successful, it's going to be through intellectual capital that creates wealth; that it's people with ideas who are making a difference. I think it's a belief that makes for greatness. Remember Walt Disney's famous dictum: "If you can dream it, you can do it." Part of leadership is magic. Remember the Grand

Inquisitor section in the *The Brothers Karamazov?* The Grand Inquisitor was angry at Christ, saying he's just involved with miracles and mystery. Well, we need miracles and mystery.

Basically, what leaders offer is intellectual capital, ideas, know-how. The key to competitive advantage is the capacity of top leadership to create a learning environment—an adaptive, agile, social architecture capable of generating intellectual capital. All the great leaders ultimately are concerned with people, dollars, and ideas. If they pick the right people, allocate the right number of dollars to particular divisions, and if they break down the bureaucratic roles so the best practices get transferred immediately from one division to the next, then we see a successful corporation. Large companies will have to try harder because they have thick walls between divisions that make passing information and ideas back and forth much more difficult.

The most successful corporations are not content to go with the status quo. General Electric, for example, was able to change without being forced, was able to reorganize and revitalize itself.

Jack Welch, CEO of General Electric, was called "Neutron Jack." The neutron bomb leaves buildings standing, but the people are gone. He's not a "Neutron Jack" today. "Look," he once said to me, "I had to be hard-nosed when I took over GE in 1981. We had 425,000 workers, and our revenue was about $25 billion. Today, our revenue is $65 billion, and we have 275,000 workers. Today, we have the companies we want and the people we want. Now I can be the coach and facilitator." He learned along the way and became a very effective leader.

Welch realized that if he wants to keep the best and the brightest, he must be the coach—the person who gets people to play at their best, who brings out the best of their ideas.

What I most admire about Jack is not just his incredible performance at GE, but this fact that he is continually reinventing himself. I once asked him what had happened to the Jack Welch who used to be known as "Neutron Jack." Now, of course, he's being called "Transformational Jack." So we talked at length about how, given changing times, he has continued to learn, to reinvent himself, to redesign and recompose his leadership style.

Leaders molt, like snakes. They shed their outside skins. But it's not just that. It's a matter of continuing to grow and showing extraordinary adaptability. Another example is James Houghton, CEO of the Corning Company. He had a human resources person who, before he retired, became Houghton's personal coach. He wanted to use the wisdom of a senior executive who had worked for his father, too, and who had some institutional history. He just wanted to continue to learn. He has evolved into an exciting leader, one who keeps reinventing or redesigning himself.

How do leaders release the brain power and creativity of people? How do they help create learning organizations? Many are evolving into confederations where decisions are made by the units that can best make them. The only reason for decisions to be made at the top is when something relates to everybody, or you need some synergy among units that can best make them. The only reason for decisions to be made at the top is when something relates to everybody, or when you need some synergy among units.

Inevitably, we will see more and more women rise to the top of organizations. Just look at the superb performance of women in all the top graduate schools of management. Women already account for over 40 percent of the enrollment in MIT, Harvard and Stanford, and their numbers have been increasing every year. We've got to stop "blaming the victim," like the title of the song from *My Fair Lady:* "Why Can't a Woman Be More Like a Man?" Who, besides Henry Higgins, would wish that on any woman? I believe that women have a natural talent for being leaders of leaders.

So many leaders have put themselves in the position where they have to regain the trust of their employees. And with all the restructuring going on today, how do leaders regain trust? Changes, particularly those that mean a reduction in jobs, are never going to be popular. However, leaders don't have to pay for change with loss of trust if their communication about change is honest, open, candid and caring. They can honestly say that they can no longer promise job security, only employability.

Another approach is to involve the employees in the restructuring so that jobs can be saved. Rather than lay off workers, Sidney Harman, president of Harman Industries, involves them in developing new uses for their products and in developing new products. For many years the company had cut perfect circles out of its round wooden speakers, and then paid a lot of money to have a trucking firm pick up thousands of these circular wood cuts, ship them off, and burn them. The employees suggested that they make clock faces out of them, because the wooden circles would be perfect clock faces. Or use them as trivets for tables, selling them in retail stores. They're also reclaiming some of the services they've been outsourcing—bringing those sources back inside, and making use of that surplus of space and people. That's creative, caring leadership.

TRICK #24

Share the Power

Although service is the paradigmatic responsibility of leaders and co-leaders, there comes a time in everyone's career when he or she asks, "What's in it for me?" Co-leaders usually lack the name recognition and enormous salaries of CEOs and others at the top, but there are rewards

For starters, serving under someone else can be a marvelous education. As a junior executive, you attend a superb college of one, where you are often able to study a first-rate leader in the flesh, day in and day out. As a vice president, you are in a unique position to study the president in office. What better curriculum for a presidential hopeful than the chance to see how the incumbent handles the duties and pressures of the office? How much better to learn from someone else's mistakes and successes before assuming that demanding position?

Some of the greatest rewards of co-leadership grow out of the relationship with the person at the top. The relationships that develop in executive offices are enormously varied. Some CEOs and COOs have healthy rivalries that energize both of them. Others have the professional equivalent of bad marriages that distract and drain them. Camaraderie grounded in shared accomplishment is one of the pleasures of any happy workplace, and it can be gratifying for the people who are most involved in setting the agenda and steering the enterprise.

Another frequent source of satisfaction for co-leaders is the opportunity to revel in interesting work and the pleasures of the craft. CEOs often barter power and responsibility for truly engaging work. It can be boring at the top, especially on days when one meeting follows another and even meals involve professional obligations. Many contented alter egos have talent or expertise that they can exercise undistracted by the top person's daunting calendar and tedious responsibilities. Successful co-leaders, especially those who decide to remain No. 2, often decide that what they do in their offices is more important than making headlines

As the happy buzz at visionary companies makes clear, the most exciting work being done today is collaborative, accomplished by teams of people working toward a common goal. In global enterprises that trade in innovation, the real power is in the hands of the men and women who have the best ideas and the most valuable skills, whatever their job titles. In the new millennium, one of the most important roles of the leader is to make sure that the necessary talent stays and is unleashed. Despite the exalted terms in which we talk about CEOs, they can actually accomplish things only when effectively teamed with other people.

LEADERSHIP REDEFINED

If we still treat some CEOs like celebrities, we are increasingly beginning to see them more as stewards than kings.

No one has been more articulate on this change in our traditional view of leadership than Peter Drucker, who said in praise of such non-imperial leaders as Harry Truman and GE's Jack Welch: "They both understood executives are not their own masters. They are servants of the organization—whether elected or appointed, whether the organization is a government, a government agency, a business, a hospital, a diocese. It's their duty to subordinate their likes, wishes, preferences to the welfare of the institution."

This view of leadership reflects a backlash against CEOs who earn far more than they deliver. The surge in executive compensation in recent years has dismayed and infuriated most people who work hard for modest pay. Corporate boards as well as workers are beginning to question if anyone deserves to make more than the budgets of entire nations.

That the workplace needs to be rethought is increasingly obvious. It is not a happy sign when the business best-seller list is topped by volumes devoted to Dilbert, the cartoon Everyworker, and the Orwellian hell in which he labors.

Although increasing numbers of firms are naming co-CEOs and showing other signs of embracing co-leadership, sharing power has its pitfalls. The corner suite that houses incompatible executive peers can be an unhappy, unproductive place. Boards can help keep the peace, but executive egos often make real partnerships impossible. Power is only shared by those who first choose to share it. In light of this, more organizations are realizing that willingness to share power is one of the criteria by which leaders must be judged.

As someone who knows both the executive experience and the subordinate one, the co-leader is a good model for a new millennium—men and women who can both command and follow, as the situation requires.

The urge to be a star and the urge to achieve common goals as part of a community have always tugged us in different directions. As celebrity becomes less associated with genuine achievement, we need to think more clearly about what is best for our organizations and for ourselves. Great co-leaders remind us that we don't need to be captain to play on the team, that doing something we want to do and doing it well can be its own reward.

ARE YOU READY TO SHARE POWER?

Executives who want to create strong, symbiotic relationships should ask themselves the following questions.

1. Can you overcome the "Superman complex," or are you too self-centered? Do you emphasize others' strengths and contributions, and not your own? Is your heart in teaming up with another high-powered talent or would you rather run the organization on your own?

2. Do your core values and philosophies mesh? How's the chemistry between the two of you?

3. Can you share the limelight, even in small ways, with your co-leader? Or do you insist on being out front on issues?

4. Are you prepared to split command with your new alter ego? Are you willing to delegate important responsibilities to him or her? Can you cut yourself loose from day-to-day affairs and cede responsibility to someone else?

5. Does your prospective co-leader have skills that truly complement yours? Or do they simply reinforce your own strengths?

6. Do you consider your second-in-command successor material? Are you fully prepared to lay out a specific career path that leads him or her to the corner office, *your* office? Do you have the patience to mentor your No. 2 personally and professionally?

7. What loyalty demands will you make on your new chief lieutenant? How will you evaluate his or her allegiance to the board of directors and other key constituencies?

8. Is the rest of the enterprise prepared to accept a strong co-leader? What's been the history with other senior executives? Will you fight for the new co-leader's success? What role will the board play?

9. Are you prepared to hear dissenting opinions? Can you tolerate constructive criticism from your top executive? Will you listen and respond positively to things you need to know but may not want to hear?

10. The ultimate test is trading places. Could you reverse roles with your new co-leader? How highly do you value his or her abilities? Is there a high degree of trust and mutual respect?

If you answered "yes" to these questions, you are probably ready to recruit a first-rate co-leader and share power.

TRICK #25

Make the Case for Co-Leaders*

An overseas visitor to our shores recently said: "If beings from another planet were trying to learn about working in the United States by reading business magazines, they would have to assume that everyone in America is either a CEO or about to become one."

The point is well taken. In *Co-Leaders,* a book I wrote with David A. Heenan, we concluded that ours is a culture obsessed with celebrity, and so we have made superstars of Bill Gates and other charismatic leaders, just as we have made legends of favored rock stars and screen actors. And, yet, even as we read yet another article that implies that Microsoft is Bill Gates, we know better. We know that every successful organization has, at its heart, a cadre of co-leaders—key players who do the work, even if they receive little of the glory.

Take Microsoft's Steve Ballmer. According to insiders, much of the software giant's unprecedented success is due to Ballmer, its relatively unknown second-in-command. President Ballmer is Microsoft's top tactician, the person responsible for everything from getting the first Windows operating system shipped to keeping the company supplied with top-notch personnel. Although the average person hears his name and wonders "Steve who?," Ballmer has created Microsoft as surely as his more famous boss has.

"Microsoft could lose Bill Gates," said former staffer Adrian King, "but it could not survive without Steve's sheer will to succeed. That's what makes the company unique."

*adapted from Co-Leaders with David Heenan, Wiley, 1999.

Our conviction is that you must look beyond Bill Gates to understand what will make organizations succeed in the new millennium. We challenge the time-honored notion that all great institutions are the lengthened shadows of a Great Man or Woman. It is a fallacy that dies hard. But if you believe, as we do, that the genius of our age is truly collaborative, you must abandon the notion that the credit for any significant achievement is solely attributable to the person at the top. We have long worshiped the imperial leader at the cost of ignoring the countless other contributors to any worthwhile enterprise. In our hearts we know that the world is more complex than ever, and that, for all but the simplest tasks, we need teams of talent—leaders and co-leaders working together—to get important things done. The old corporate monotheism is finally giving way to a more realistic view that acknowledges leaders, not as organizational gods, but as the first among many contributors. In this new view of the organization, co-leaders finally come into their own and begin to receive the credit they so richly deserve.

Gates and Ballmer exemplify a relatively new type of alliance between a leader and his or her chief ally. In these lash-ups, so typical of Silicon Valley, the No. 1 and No. 2 seem more like buddies, or at least like peers, than boss and subordinate. This new egalitarianism reflects a dramatic change in organizational life in the New Economy. In the corporate America of Henry Ford, the person at the top held all the power. He, and it was almost always a he, owned the company and all its assets. The workers were hired hands.

But on the cusp of the Year 2000, economics is based on a very different reality. Microsoft and other knowledge-oriented companies are in the business of ideas. Good ideas belong, initially at least, to whoever has them, not to the company or the boss. Superior ideas can come from anyone in the organization, and they empower the people who have them, whether their business card says CEO or intern. If Microsoft is not a true meritocracy, it is nonetheless still a company in which talent is valued and courted. Talent always has the power to walk (especially if, as in the case of Ballmer, the talent already has roughly $13 billion worth of Microsoft stock in its pocket). In such an environment, no chief executive would risk losing a key player by demanding unquestioning obedience or any of the other outdated perks of the rigidly hierarchical corporation of yesterday. This new egalitarianism isn't just a matter of style. It's a question of survival. In the new climate, every leader knows that the organization's best minds will take major assets with them, should they walk out the door.

CO-LEADERSHIP DEFINED

Co-leadership is not a fuzzy-minded buzzword designed to make non-CEOs feel better about themselves and their workplaces. Rather, it is a tough-minded strategy that will unleash the hidden talent in every enterprise. Above all, co-leadership is inclusive, not exclusive. It celebrates those who do the real work, not just a few charismatic leaders, often isolated, who are regally compensated for articulating the organization's vision.

Although several leading companies from Citigroup to DaimlerChrysler have re-jigged themselves around "co-equal" CEOs, co-leadership should permeate every organization at every level. There are vivid demonstrations of successful power sharing from the Halls of Montezuma to the Hills of Silicon Valley. For example, the United States Marine Corps, with its fiercely proud tradition of excellence in combat and its unbending code of honor, exemplifies co-leadership. Despite its rigid command-and-control structure, the Corps' enduring culture screams togetherness: Semper Fi. Esprit de corps. The few, the proud.

Such inclusive notions of leadership are not new. The Marines have been practicing their special brand of esprit for more than 220 years. But what is new are the changed realities of the twenty-first century. In a world of increasing interdependence and ceaseless technological change, even the greatest of Great Men or Women simply can't get the job done alone. As a result, we need to rethink our most basic concepts of leadership.

We spent five years scrutinizing dozens of gifted co-leaders, analyzing how they contributed to the greatness of their organizations. No one illustrates the co-star better than George Catlett

Marshall. As important to his country as George Washington, Marshall brought unprecedented stature to a supporting role. With World War II looming, he rebuilt the United States Army despite extraordinary initial resistance. The architect of the Marshall Plan, he was President Truman's steady right hand as secretary of state and later secretary of defense. The first soldier to win the Nobel Peace Prize in peacetime, he was also a hero to the captains of his era. Truman, Eisenhower, and Churchill all said he was the greatest man they had ever known.

Routinely called upon to do the work and forego the credit, great lieutenants sometimes have character where more celebrated leaders have only flash. Marshall is, again, the model. In retirement, he turned down million-dollar offers to write his memoirs because he felt his reminiscences might trouble some of the people in his remarkable past.

Co-leaders, including such contemporary standouts as Microsoft's Ballmer, Intel's Craig Barnett, and America Online's Robert Pittman, illustrate how the once yawning gap between the person at the top and the rest of the organization is closing because of rapid changes in the workplace and, indeed, the world. Although, as a culture, we continue to be mesmerized by celebrity and preoccupied with being No. 1, the roles of top executives are converging, the line between them increasingly blurred.

Called upon to make more and more complex decisions more and more quickly, the most da Vincian CEOs acknowledge that they can't do everything themselves. Far-sighted corporations, universities, and other organizations require their leaders to do more than put effective systems in place. Future-oriented enterprises are like viruses, constantly changing in response to shifts in the global environment. As a result, the CEO's job doesn't get easier the longer he or she is in place; it typically gets even more demanding.

The untimely death in 1997 of Coca-Cola CEO Roberto Goizueta reminded the world that no complex organization can afford to rely too heavily on a single leader, however gifted and charismatic. Coke never stumbled in the days following Goizueta's death, largely because he had already groomed an able successor, M. Douglas Ivester, whom Goizueta had long referred to as "my partner." The company's major divisions were already reporting to Ivester, now CEO, when the Cuban-born chief became ill. The late chairman had also nurtured a dozen more key players under Ivester, who, in turn, had talented proteges of his own, called "Doug-ettes." In famed investor Warren Buffett's view, Goizueta's "greatest legacy is the way he so carefully selected and then nurtured the future leadership of the company."

Contrast, too, China's smooth leadership transition with the sorry state of Russia, Cuba and Indonesia. Deng Xiaoping's death quickly surfaced two talented co-leaders: President Jiang Zemin and Premier Zhu Rongji. Yet Russia, with Boris Yeltsin acting more like a tsar than the country's first democratically elected president, desperately needs a succession plan. So, too, do autocratic Cuba and beleaguered Indonesia. Increasingly, countries, companies, and other entities are realizing that top leaders and their co-leaders are not different orders of beings, but essential complements: All are needed if the enterprise is to flourish.

PATHS TO CO-LEADERSHIP

In studying outstanding lieutenants we were constantly reminded that co-leadership is a role, not an identity, and certainly not a destiny. There is no single personality type that consigns people to careers in a supporting role rather than a starring one (indeed most CEOs and other leaders have done both). True, some strong-willed individuals must run their own shows. It's hard—almost impossible, actually—to imagine Donald Trump, George Steinbrenner, or Leona Helmsley finding happiness in the trenches. But they are the exceptions.

Since all leadership is situational, we are leery about categorizing co-leaders. The social world isn't nearly as orderly as the physical world. People—unlike solids, fluids, and gases—are anything but uniform and predictable. We can find successful co-leaders in every field of endeavor. But in the course of our research, we found that, however they differed, each had taken one of three distinctive career paths to successful co-leadership. Each was either a fasttracker, a back-tracker, or an on-tracker.

Fast-trackers are deputies on the way up. For presidential wannabe Al Gore and others, co-leadership is a rite of passage. Indeed, being No. 2 is a time-honored way to become top dog. According to a recent survey, 86 percent of the heads of Fortune 500 companies were previous chief operating officers.

Upwardly mobile lieutenants understand that the route to the corner office is paved with achievement, loyalty and luck. Savvy deputies also appreciate first-hand the need for superior bench strength. Fast-trackers tend to be good at what psychologist Erik Erikson terms, 'being generative"—that is, building their own cadre of talented lieutenants. Such co-leaders often understand, in the most visceral way, the value of sharing power.

Back-trackers are former chief executives who have down-shifted. one of history's most notable examples is Chou Enlai, who voluntarily relinquished command of the Red Army to a gifted junior officer, Mao Tse-tung. More recently, as few would have predicted, colorful cable pioneer Ted Turner seems to have found happiness as a vice chairman at Time Warner.

Some back-trackers disdain elements of the No. 1 role: deal-making, strategizing, schmoozing with different interest groups, and the like. Some find the pressure and lack of privacy at the top to be major negatives. Others want to avoid the nerve-rattling revolving-door syndrome of today's executive suite. Generally speaking, these talented men and women find greater peace-of-mind being the quiet power behind the throne.

On-trackers are outstanding adjuncts who either didn't want the top slot or weren't promoted into it. These people find ways to prosper as supporting players. Passed over for CEO of Chrysler, Bob Lutz calls his stint as second-in-command "absolutely the best period in my whole career." On-trackers have the ego strength to be a co-star. If they are offered top billing, they will probably take it, as Harry Truman did a half century ago. But they are also comfortable remaining part of a vibrant team of leaders.

Whatever their route to co-leadership, successful co-stars are consummate team players and, thus, valuable models for every-one interested in effective collaboration. Usually servant-leaders, they tend to be self-reliant, yet committed to organizational goals. Outstanding co-leaders "see themselves—except in terms of line responsibility—as equals to the leaders they follow," says Professor Robert E. Kelley of Carnegie Mellon University. "They are apt to disagree openly with leadership and are less likely to be intimidated by hierarchy and organizational structure."

SHARING THE LIMELIGHT

To be a successful co-leader, you need, above everything else, a champion who will allow you to succeed. Not every top gun is able to do that.

Contrast Bob Lutz's success as president (and, later, vice chairman) of Chrysler, thanks to the genuine partnership he had with CEO Robert Eaton, with Lutz's unhappiness at the auto giant when then CEO Lee Iacocca often undermined him. Great co-leaders are often born when leaders decide to do the one thing that most often distinguishes a great organization from a mediocre one—hiring people who are as good or better than they are. As low profile as Lutz is flamboyant, Eaton was perfectly comfortable with a deputy who piloted his own jet fighter and who was a darling of the press. For Lutz's part, he long ago came to terms with being passed over for Chrysler's top job and found real happiness as Eaton's partner in everything but name. Indeed, Lutz believes Eaton's willingness to share power was key to Chrysler's success. If Lutz had been made CEO in 1992, he said: "I would have had to have done it alone."

True leaders also know that the only deputies worth hiring are the ones good enough to replace them. And, for their part, outstanding co-leaders know that they don't have to be at the top of the organizational chart to find satisfaction—that exercising one's gifts and serving a worthy cause are far more reliable sources of satisfaction than the title on one's office door. Such men and women have acquired the ability, rare in this culture, to distinguish between celebrity and success. As that unlikely philosopher, the late Erma Bombeck, once wrote, "Don't confuse fame with success. Madonna is one, Helen Keller is the other."

Courage is one of the attributes of all great co-leaders, and one we rarely associate with that role. Deputies have to be able to speak truth to power, even when it hurts. (Real leaders demand honesty from their adjuncts, knowing that good information, even when it's unpleasant, is the basis of good decision making.) It was young George Marshall's courage in publicly correcting Gen. "Black Jack" Pershing that caught Pershing's eye and launched Marshall's extraordinary career. And candor like his own was one of the attributes Marshall always sought in his staffers. Yes-men may feed the boss's ego, but they serve no other useful function. Indeed, they guarantee that the boss's knowledge will be limited to upbeat information and whatever he or she already knows. Good co-leaders protect their bosses when possible, but good bosses are willing to endure occasional discomfiture in order to find out what they need to know.

Every chief has the right to the loyalty of his or her deputies. Working at a leader's side, a trusted co-leader is often privy to information that could seriously compromise the boss's position if it were shared. As candid as good adjuncts are in private, they are equally discreet in public. They can keep the boss's secrets—as long as they can continue to reconcile them with their own consciences. To some extent, all No. 1's depend on an image of excellence to maintain their positions. Good co-leaders may know about personal flaws or weaknesses, but they don't feel compelled to reveal them or underscore them. Especially in crises, leaders have to know that their first lieutenants will maintain the illusion of superiority that makes leadership possible. An exemplary instance of this is Vice President Al Gore's unswerving public loyalty to his bruised top banana, despite the pressure on Gore to distance himself from the rakish president as Gore himself seeks the nation's highest office.

Co-leaders need unusually healthy egos. That's a paradox, really, since it would seem that they would need less ego strength than the person in the corner office. But, especially in a society as obsessed with winning as ours, it takes extraordinary confidence to be No. 2 or No. 3. No matter how great a contribution a great co-leader makes, the majority of the credit is going to accrue to the top dog. That's the nature of the organizational beast. To some degree, it may simply reflect the extent to which leaders function as symbols of their enterprises. But the fact is that even the best deputy will exist in the shadow of the boss.

What does the organization get from a first-rate co-leader? A great many things. Two heads really are better than one when it comes to decision making. The psychological literature indicates that groups make better choices than individuals do. A first-rate colleague can serve as an alternative model for the rest of the organization, one that other co-leaders may relate to more easily than to the person at the top. A great deputy can serve as institutional insurance in that he or she can quickly get up to speed to replace the person at the top. This is, tragically, one of the roles American vice presidents have had to play when presidents have died in office, and it is the role that most people measure the vice president by Truman, whom, as vice president, FDR had kept in the dark about many important issues, including the development of the atomic bomb, proved surprisingly able in the nation's top job. The very thought of Dan Quayle succeeding George Bush so frightened many voters that it became a factor in Bush's failure to win a second term in office.

But heir apparent is just one of the many roles co-leaders play. Great lieutenants may have strengths and skills that the boss lacks. The co-star can compensate or complement. William Clark had superior cartographic abilities to Meriwether Lewis, for instance, that proved invaluable to the Corps of Discovery. More recently, Berkshire Hathaway Vice Chairman Charles Munger has become known as the man behind Warren Buffett's magic touch. The Los Angeles-based attorney has been so good at goading Buffett out of borderline investments that he calls Munger "the abominable no man." Two-high powered brains in sync can share the burden of leadership and lighten the workload. Co-leaders routinely act as facilitators for their superiors. They almost always serve as advisors as well, at best, providing the kind of candid, informed counsel that every leader needs. They are often conduits of critical information from elsewhere in the organization to the person in charge and vice versa. They can also serve as sounding boards, counselors, confessors and pressure valves. In bad times, they may serve as lightning rods, even scapegoats.

In the best of all possible organizations, they are partners, though not necessarily equal ones, sharing responsibilities with the chief according to their individual skills and interests. In the highly collaborative Clinton White House, Gore assumed major policy-shaping responsibility for several areas of national and international concern, including national security, environment and technology.

Two Heads Are Better Than One—Sometimes

To build strength at the top, some firms are opting for a more radical (and, possibly, riskier) approach to co-leadership. They are formalizing their commitment to power sharing by appointing co-equals to the corner office. Among those companies: Unilever, Warner Bros., J. C. Penney Co., Ralston Purina Co., and software server Sapient Corp. However, the financial services sector is probably the most taken with the two-for-one trend.

At Charles Schwab Corp., the San Francisco-based discount brokerage, David S. Pottruck, its president and COO, shares the title of chief executive officer with company founder, Charles Schwab. As co-CEO, Pottruck says Schwab will continue to serve as the company's "visionary," while Pottruck will focus more on strategy and day-to-day operations. Back East, Goldman, Sachs has had two pairs of co-CEOs. Morgan Stanley, Dean Witter & Discover Co. is run jointly by CEO Philip J. Purcell and President John J. Mack, although Purcell technically outranks Mack. Chase Manhattan Bank also adopted a tandem approach to leadership. However, Chase's cross-town rival, Citicorp, has turned the most heads by teaming up with Travelers Group Inc. Pending regulatory approval, the newly christened Citigroup Inc. will be the world's largest financial-services company, with assets of nearly $80 billion. Sharing command of the financial powerhouse: co-CEOs John S. Reed from Citicorp and Travelers' Sanford I. Weill.

Meshing a commercial bank (Citicorp) with an investment bank and insurer (Travelers) will be difficult enough. Sharing power in the executive suite may be even more challenging. Reed and Weill are used to running their own shows, and they have strikingly different personalities. Reed, who grew up in Argentina and Brazil (he is fluent in Spanish and Portuguese) has global and cerebral interests. An engineer by training and a classic buttoned-down banker, Reed is a very private person, who, as an executive, is more interested in the big picture than nitty-gritty details. Brooklyn-born Weill, on the other hand, is gregarious and outgoing—a people guy. Entrepreneurial and street smart, Weill often relies on intuition over analysis. The consummate hands-on manager, he tends to be less keen on strategizing than in getting things done.

Will this Odd Couple work? So far, Reed and Weill are saying, and doing, everything right. The reconfigured Citigroup board has equal numbers of Reed people and Weill people—a good first step toward keeping power balanced in the corner suite. Moreover, both men speak respectfully of the teams of co-leaders the other had put together before the merger. That kind of mutual respect goes far to keep in check the organization's inevitable post-merger paranoia. Neither man is talking about stepping aside or down any time soon.

If the co-CEO structure is to work, Reed and Weill will have to believe that they can make more of Citigroup together than they can separately. Clearly, the challenges of teaming such strong personalities are considerable. Conflicts inevitably arise, and egos must always be added into the equation. As one cynic, Michael Feuer, founder and CEO of OfficeMax, Inc., puts it: "If two chief executives think they can share power, they've been reading too much 'Goldilocks and The Three Bears.'"

The jury is still out on dual CEOs. But we do know that successful co-leadership cultures depend on mind-set and commitment. The true test of co-leadership is always the No. 1's willingness to share power with a potential ally. The accelerating trend toward mega-mergers, even global mergers, no doubt means there will be more co-CEOs in the future. The very existence of tandem leadership sends a powerful message that successful organizations are collections of talent, not solely reflections of the genius of the CEO, however gifted.

TRICK # 26

Create Leaders at Every Level*

Where have all the leaders gone? The quick answer is that the cost of ambition and the cost of a position of leadership is beyond what people are willing to pay. When you think about the presidential race and the potential nominees—the people who are interested in running—it's a rather meager group.

The demands on the role in both the public and private sector, the attention from the media, the increased complexity of the world—the globalization, the galloping technology—make leadership infinitely more difficult. I think there's a general tendency of a dyspeptic mood toward institutional leaders. It's part of the American paranoid style. But I think it's been exacerbated in recent years given the kind of scandals going on, the media attention, the questions about character—the complexity, the media attention, the price you pay for the kinds of demands executives now have.

Just look at the role of chief executives. To do their job, they work an 80 to 100 hour week. Who needs that? For all those reasons, people are just sort of shying away from top leadership—and often the people who need power to live are unfortunately the ones who end up in the top jobs. "Never give power to a person who can't live without it," said my father. So that's what we have going up. We have Richard III, not George Washington.

I think it's a different issue in middle management. At the middle level, most organizations in all three sectors—governmental, not-for-profit and for-profit—do not create cultures that would encourage people to take initiative and then lead. It's not rewarded.

adapted from Co-Leaders with David Heenan, Wiley, 1999.

They give employees very little sense of the skills that would help make them better leaders. They don't identify the terrific coaches— and if they ever did, they wouldn't reward them.

There's all sorts of things at the middle level which, at best, don't discourage leadership. But in very few cases are there programs to encourage it. It's either ignored or not rewarded. There's a bureaucratization of initiative that occurs at the middle management level which is very serious.

And that is at the organization's expense. Leadership at the mid-level is something they should give more attention to. Otherwise they'll back into the future, not walk into it. Without good leaders in this incredibly complicated world, they're just going to be out of business in a while.

Given the kind of spastic, volatile environment we live in, I think leadership must make a profound difference. If you look at the organizations that fail, it's almost always due to a lack of leadership at all levels. Most organizations don't encourage leaders at every level.

Leadership is really a matter of character. The process of becoming a leader is no different than the process of becoming a fully integrated, healthy human being.

I like to ask not just the question "What should leaders do in service to their constituencies?" but the inverse: "What do people want from their leaders?" I find that people want four things, four competencies: (1) they want direction and meaning—a sense of purpose, a vision, a set of beliefs and convictions; (2) they want leaders to generate and sustain trust; (3) they want leaders to be purveyors of hope and optimism because they have to buy into the future; and (4) they want results. Those four things are universally wanted by people in all institutions. Leaders provide those four competencies. Those are the main qualities of leadership.

To a great extent, I think it's life experiences that generally shape our capacity for leadership. It's not a Ph.D. or an MBA. The only initials that really count are L.I.F.E.—what we experience on the job. I don't think it's fruitful to argue whether it's born or made. The point is everybody can improve.

We are still in our infancy stages of understanding what helps develop leaders: How to learn things like leadership. Or learn how to have a good marriage—be a good parent. All of those things we pick up from the environment—and the major environment where we pick up things about leading comes from our organizations.

There are two ways of learning about leadership. One is personally and one is organizationally. Personally, individuals should reflect on their own experiences. One way to do this is by keeping a diary. It's also important to get feedback on how you're doing from people whose opinions and values you trust. Organizationally, people learn about leadership based on who gets ahead in the organization. Promote the wrong people into positions of leadership, and you send a myriad of wrong messages.

Ease Tension by Being Authentic

I continue to sense the tension in organizations between personal actualization and freedom and the achievement of organizational goals. I think that business should model science in its respect for dissent and its commitment to experimentation and collaboration. I am more interested than ever in creative collaboration, the process whereby a group pools talents and creates something that transcends the contribution of the individuals.

Tomorrow's organizations will be federations, networks, clusters, cross-functional teams, temporary systems, ad hoc task forces, lattices, modules, matrices—almost anything but pyramids. The successful ones will make problem finding, not problem solving, their first priority. They will be led by people who embrace error, even occasional failure, because they know it will teach them more than success. Such organizations will be led by people who understand the primal pleasure of the hunt that is problem solving.

In the 21st century, the laurel will go to the leader who encourages healthy dissent and values those followers courageous enough to say no. It will go to the leader who exults in cultural differences and knows that diversity is the best hope for long-term survival. These new leaders will not have the loudest voice, but the most attentive ear. These men and women will build organizations of energy and ideas. They will find their joy in the task at hand, not in leaving monuments behind as "legacies."

Once in Boston, a foreign visitor walked up to a sailor and asked why American ships were built to last only a short time. According to the tourist, "The sailor answered without hesitation that the art of navigation is making such rapid progress that the finest ship would become obsolete if it lasted beyond a few years. In these words, I began to recognize the general and systematic idea upon which your great people direct all their concerns."

The foreign visitor was that shrewd observer of American morals and manners, Alexis de Tocqueville, and the year was 1835. He had captured the central theme of our country: its preoccupation, its obsession with change. One thing is new, however, since de Tocqueville's time: the acceleration of newness, the changing scale and scope of change. As Dr. Robert Oppenheimer said, "The world alters as we walk in it. The years of our lives measure not some small growth or moderation of what we learned in childhood, but a great upheaval."

NEW PHILOSOPHY

The shift in spiritual values stems from the need, not only to humanize the organization but to use it as a crucible of personal growth and self-realization. I suspect that the desire for relationships in business has little to do with a profit motive, and more to do with our quest for self-awareness, to achieve and stretch our potentialities and possibilities. This deliberate self-analysis has spread to organizations, where there has been a dramatic upsurge of this spirit of inquiry. At new depths and over a wider range, organizations are opening their operations to self-inquiry and self-analysis, which involves a change in how the people who make history and those who make knowledge regard each other. The scientists have realized their affinity with men and women of affairs, and the latter have found a new receptivity and respect for men and women of knowledge.

This deliberate and self-conscious examination of organizational behavior has resulted in more collaborative relationships to improve performance. This new form of collaboration features unprecedented reciprocity between managers and workers Never before have business leaders so willingly searched, scrutinized, examined, inspected, or contemplated for meaning, for purpose, for improvement. Managers have had to shake off old prejudices about certain people and make themselves and their organizations vulnerable and receptive to external sources and new, unexpected, even unwanted information.

How can our needs be reconciled with the needs and goals of our employing organizations? How can individual needs and organizational goals be integrated? Is the conflict between individual needs (like spending time with the family) and organizational demands (like meeting deadlines) inescapable? Under conditions of constant change, I see a much deeper understanding of human complexity emerging. Today, integration encompasses the entire range of issues concerned with individual incentives, rewards, and motivations, and organizational success. In our society, where personal attachments play an important role, the individual is appreciated, and there is genuine concern for his well-being, not just in a hygiene sense, but as a moral, integrated personality.

This problem is one of power and of how power is distributed. It is a complex issue and alive with controversy. The power of leaders has to be seriously considered because of dramatic changes that make the possibility of one-man rule not necessarily "bad" but impractical. Peter Drucker listed 41 major responsibilities of the CEO and declared that "90 percent of the trouble we are having with the chief executive's job is rooted in our superstition of the one-man chief." Many factors make one-man control obsolete, among them the broadening product base of industry; the impact of new technology; the scope of international operations; the separation of management from ownership; the rise of trade unions; and the dissemination of general education. The real power of the chief has been eroding. Concentrating power at the top, perhaps in one person who has the knowledge and resources to control the entire enterprise, may be the perfect way to run a railroad and to manage routine tasks, but it is not suitable to leading in a rapidly changing, turbulent, unpredictable climate. I see a deepening interdependence among stakeholders. Businesses are increasingly enmeshed in legislation and public policy. Government will be more involved more of the time. Maximizing cooperation rather than competition among organizations, particularly if their fates are correlated, may be a strong possibility.

This problem of managing and resolving conflicts grows out of the same conflicts and stereotypes that divide nations and communities. As organizations become more complex, they fragment and divide, building tribal patterns and symbolic codes, which often work to exclude others (secrets and jargon, for example) and on occasion to exploit differences for inward (and always fragile) harmony. While it is simple to induce conflict, it is difficult to arrest it. When two groups of people who have never been together are given a task that will be judged by an impartial jury, in less than one hour, each group devolves into a tightly knit band with all the symptoms of an "in" group. They regard their product as a "masterwork" and the other group's as commonplace at best. "Other" becomes "enemy." "We are good, they are bad; we are right, they are wrong." Modern organizations abound with bands of specialists held together by the illusion of a unique identity who tend to view others with suspicion.

In organizations, the problem of identity is manifest in how clear and committed the organization is to its goals. Modern organizations are extremely vulnerable to an identity problem, chiefly because rapid growth and turbulence transform and distort the original, simpler goals. Complexity and diversity lead to different orientations within subsystems. Goals that may be clear within one system may be seen as antithetical, or at best only vaguely understood, by other subsystems. Constant surveillance of the primary tasks is necessary.

Leaders must embrace ideas that engender buoyancy, resilience, and a fearlessness of revision. I find that the elements of revitalization are an ability to learn from experience and to codify, store, and retrieve the relevant knowledge; an ability to acquire and use feedback on performance, in short, to be self-analytical; and an ability to direct one's own destiny. These qualities have much in common with self-renewal.

In the first two decades of the 21st century, rapid technological change and diversification will lead to more and more partnerships between government and business. It will be a truly mixed economy. Because of the immensity and expense of the projects, there will be fewer identical units competing in the same markets, and organizations will become more interdependent. The four main features of this environment are interdependence rather than competition; turbulence and uncertainty rather than readiness and certainty; large-scale rather than small-scale enterprises; and complex and multinational rather than simple national enterprises

Continuing education will become the distinctive characteristic of the new culture. Adult education is growing fast because of the rate of professional obsolescence. The average engineer requires further education only 10 years after getting his degree. It will be almost routine for the experienced physician, engineer, and executive to go back to school for advanced training every two or three years. All of this education is not just "nice" but necessary.

The ease of transportation, coupled with the needs of a dynamic environment, change drastically the ideas of owning a job or having roots. The increased level of education and mobility will change the values we place on work. People will be more intellectually committed to their jobs and will probably require more involvement, participation, and autonomy. Also, people will be more "other-oriented," taking cues for their norms and values from their immediate environment rather than tradition.

The tasks of the organization will be too complicated for one person to comprehend, to say nothing of control. Essentially, they will call for the collaboration of specialists in a project or a team form of organization. Business will increasingly concern itself with its adaptive or innovative-creative capacity.

The structure of organizations of the future will be temporary. There will be adaptive, rapidly changing, temporary systems. These will be task forces organized around problems to be solved by groups of relative strangers with diverse professional skills. The group will be arranged on an organic model; it will evolve in response to a problem rather than to programmed role expectations. The leader will become the coordinator or "linking pin" between various task forces. He or she must have the skills to relay information and to mediate between groups. People will be evaluated not according to rank but according to skill and professional training. Organizational charts will consist of project groups rather than stratified functional groups. Adaptive, problem-solving, temporary systems of diverse specialists, linked together by coordinating and task-evaluating executive specialists in an organic flux—these adaptive structures will not only reduce intergroup conflicts, they may also induce honest-to-goodness creative collaboration.

Adaptive leaders increase motivation and effectiveness, because they create conditions under which individuals can gain increased satisfaction. There should be a harmony between the educated individual's need for tasks that are meaningful, satisfying, and creative and an adaptive organizational structure.

Accompanying the increased integration between individual and organizational goals will be new modes of relating and changing commitments to work groups. The peer group at work significantly impacts performance and morale. The work group creates and reinforces norms and standards, from the number of units produced to the interaction and intimacy, communication, control, and regulation of behavior. But in the new adaptive organizations, many work groups will be temporary systems, so people must learn to develop intense relationships on the job and learn to bear the absence of more enduring work relationships. We should expect to experience a concentration of emotional energy in forming relationships quickly and intensely and then a dissolution and rapid relocation of personal attachments—emotional acrobatics.

More time and energy will have to be spent on continual rediscovery of the appropriate mix of people, competencies, and tasks within an ambiguous and unstructured existence.

The future I describe is not necessarily a "happy" one. Coping with rapid change, living in temporary work systems, developing meaningful relations and then breaking them—all augur social strains and psychological tensions. Teaching how to live with ambiguity, to identify with the adaptive process, to make a virtue out of contingency, and to be self-directing—these will be the tasks of education, the goals of maturity, and the achievement of the successful individual.

In these new organizations, participants will be called upon to use their minds more. Fantasy, imagination, and creativity will be legitimate in ways that today seem strange. Social structures will no longer be instruments of psychic repression but will increasingly promote play and freedom on behalf of curiosity and thought.

Two trends today further reflect the need for more openness. One is the radical assault women are making today on the traditional male ineptness at emotional communication. In the past this defect was considered a virtue, and the masculine tradition of stumbling around mutely, weighted down with a crippling load of grim psychological armor, was an unquestioned tenet of the patriarchal status quo. Today it is in retreat as men are less willing to pay the price of emotional strangulation. As women enter the workforce in large numbers—many simply from economic need but many by preference—the notion of one partner "outgrowing" the other applies with even greater force to women who "find themselves" in a professional career, and discover that their husbands have lost relevance in the process. A second trend is the prevalence in the media of what might be called foible comedy— the expression and exposure for comic recognition of the most petty and ignominious human impulses—those thoughts and feelings we are most likely to hide from others. The long-running popularity of Seinfeld, for example, may well be due to its relentless verbalization of thoughts and feelings we all share and usually refuse to admit, even to ourselves. The laughter it provokes is not only cleansing but liberating, for it says to share these foibles is to be human, and trying to hide them a waste of energy.

A TIME OF TRANSITION

We are in a period of transition between an old system and a new one and every strain and discomfort is heightened by comparison with old assumptions. But people are amazingly adaptable and creative, and new systems are in the process of evolving.

For example, on one company bulletin board, I saw this chart:

We can't tell you how long we'll be in business.
We can't promise we won't be bought by another company.
We can't promise there will be room for promotion.
We can't promise you a job until retirement age.
We can't promise there will be money for your pension.
We can't expect your undying loyalty, and we aren't sure
we want it.

In such a hostile climate, the leader must show competence, constancy, caring, candor, and congruity. Where there is hope, there is life, even optimism that we can find ways around any problem. We can learn to think of failures as the result of using the wrong strategies, not the result of some character flaw. We can keep past successes in mind. Our success, after all, does not rest upon infallible judgments but on the courage to experiment and the ability to learn from mistakes. Experimentation, even taking into account the experiments that do not succeed, is, in the long run, safer than too great caution.

We see the transition from one paradigm to another.

From Earlier Paradigm:	*To Current and Future Paradigm:*
Focusing on numbers and tasks	Focusing on quality, service, and the customer
Confronting and Combating	Collaborating and Unifying
Stressing independence	Fostering interdependence
Encouraging "old boy" networks	Respecting, honoring, and leveraging diversity
Changing by necessity and crisis	Continuously learning and innovating
Being internally competitive	Being globally competitive
Having a narrow focus: "Me and my organization"	Having a broader focus: "My community, my society, my world"

In many ways, it's a whole new ball game. As Rosabeth Moss Kanter wrote: "The new game brings with it a new challenge. The mad rush to improve performance and to pursue excellence has caused the number of demands on executives and managers to escalate. These demands come from every part of business and personal life, and they increasingly seem incompatible and impossible."

Indeed, among those conflicting demands, she cites the following: Think strategically and invest in the future—but keep the numbers up today. Be entrepreneurial and take risks—but don't cost the business anything by failing. Continue to do everything you're doing even better—and spend more time communicating with employees, serving on teams, and launching new projects. Know every detail of your business—but delegate more responsibility to others. Become passionately dedicated to "visions" and fanatically committed to carrying them out—but be flexible, responsive, and able to change direction quickly. Speak up, be a leader, set the direction—but be participative, listen well, co-operate. Throw yourself wholeheartedly into the entrepreneurial game and the long hours it takes—but stay fit and raise terrific children.

Organizations, too, face escalating and seemingly incompatible demands: Get lean and mean through restructuring—while being a great company to work for and offering employee-centered policies like job security. Encourage creativity and innovation to take you in new directions—but stick to your core competencies. Communicate a sense of urgency and push for faster execution, faster results—but take time to deliberately plan for the future. Decentralize to delegate profit and planning responsibilities to small, autonomous business units—but centralize to capture synergies and efficiencies and combine resources in innovative ways.

So, in light of these conflicting demands, how's a person to cope? Rather than simply administer, imitate, and maintain—innovate and originate. Rather than focus on structure, focus on people; rather than rely on control, inspire trust; rather than have a short-range perspective, have a long-range vision; rather than accept the status quo, ask questions.

In all honesty, if I hadn't seen several exemplary and courageous leaders make major changes in themselves and in their organizations for the better, I don't know that I would believe them to be possible. As Robert D. Haas, chairman and CEO of The Levi Strauss Co. notes: "It's difficult to unlearn behaviors that made us successful in the past. Speaking rather than listening. Valuing people like yourself over people of different genders or from different cultures. Doing things on your own rather than collaborating. Making the decision yourself instead of asking different people for their perspectives. There's a whole range of behaviors that were highly functional in the old hierarchal organization that are dead wrong in the flatter, more responsive empowered organization that we're seeking to become."

Exemplary leaders provide what their constituents need.

In Service of Constituent Needs	*Leaders Provide*	*To Help Create*
Direction/Meaning	Purpose	Goals and Objectives
Trust	Integrity/Authenticity	Reliability and Consistency
Hope	Optimism	Energy and Commitment
Results	Bias Toward Action	Confidence and Creativity

In conclusion, I quote Stephen Sondheim's lyrics from "Sunday in the Park with George."

A vision's just a vision if it's only in your head.
If no one gets to hear it, it's as good as dead.
It has to come to life.
Bit by bit, putting it together . . .
Piece by piece, only way to make a work of art.
Every moment makes a contribution,
Every little detail plays a part.
Having just the visions's no solution
Everything depends of execution,
Putting it together, that's what counts.

APPENDIX

A

action, 51, 55
adaptability, 141
adaptation, 123-24
administration, dual, 94
alchemy, 83
alienation, 31, 82
Allen, Bob, 39
alliance, sense of, 14
ambiguity, 180
ambition, 29
America Online, 162
Anderson Consulting,
    108, 109-10
Apple Computer, 24, 66-
    67, 78, 84, 97
approach, systemic, 136
architecture, social,
    109-10
arrogance, 84
Asea Brown Boveri
    (ABB), 78, 107
assets, people as, 112
assignments,
    international, 103
AT&T, 39, 132
atomic bomb, 167
authoritarianism, 140,
    142, 146
autocrats, 119
autonomy, 57, 179

B

backtalk, reflective, 55
backtrackers, 163-64
Ballmer, Steve, 159, 162
Barnard, Chester, 125
Barnett, Craig, 162
Barnevik, Percy, 58, 78,
    107
beliefs, 172
benchmark, developing a,
    75-76
Ben and Jerry's, 114
Benetton, 57

Biederman, Patricia
    Ward, 66, 69
Black Mountain
    College, 96
blacks, success of, 142
Body Shop, The, 114
Bombeck, Erma, 165
bowling analogy, 82
bureaucracy, 56, 59, 65,
    99
belonging, sense of,
    13-14
Blair, Tony, 22
body, life of the, 18
Bohr, Niels, 98
bottom line, 64
boundaries, 52
Boveri, Asea Brown, 58
Bradlee, Ben, 103
brainpower, 107
    misuse of, 110-11
Buffett, Warren, 163,
    167
Burger King, 100
Burke, Jim, 26
Bush, George, 22, 167

C

Cage, John, 118
CalFed, 132
candor, 34, 166, 182
capability, 74
capital, intellectual, 66,
    90, 107, 150
capitalism, 115
caring, 33, 73, 182
Carlyle, Thomas, 19
Carlzon, Jan, 27, 131,
    132
cause, having a, 100
CEOs, 10, 28, 65, 133,
    155-56, 162
    canonization of, 81
    disparity of wealth of,
    115
    reinvention of, 149

change, 82, 108
    consequences of, 116
    constancy of, 119,
    144-45
    embracing, 139
    openness to, 123
    rate of, 97
    stability and, 124
    technology and, 101
Chaos Theory, 140
character, 19, 34-36, 76
    and competence, 32
    and judgment, 36
    leaders and, 51, 172
charisma, 17
Chase Manhattan
    Bank, 168
chat rooms, 49
chauvinism, male, 53
China, 82
Chrysler, 164-65
Citigroup, 161, 168
civility, 142
Clark, William, 167
Clinton, Bill, 22, 29,
    99, 166
closure, 64
coaching, 77, 103, 151
Coca-Cola, 23, 56-58,
    100, 162
cohesiveness, 127
co-leaders, 155, 157
collaboration, 52, 70,
    98, 150, 156, 176
    building, 122
    creative, 93, 95-96,
    108, 111, 180
    effective, 164
    of genius, 160
    technology and, 82
command-and-control,
    83
commitment, 38, 117,
    179
    shared, 46

ABOUT THE AUTHOR

Warren Bennis is Distinguished Professor of Business Administration and Founding Chairman of The Leadership Institute at the University of Southern California. He has been observing and writing about leaders and managers for more than four decades. His many books include the best-selling *Leaders* and *On Becoming a Leader,* the Pulitzer Prize-nominated *An Invented Life, Organizing Genius,* and *Managing People Is Like Herding Cats.*

Bennis has served on the faculties of MIT's Sloan School of Management, Harvard University, and Boston University, and he has been executive vice president of the State University of New York at Buffalo and president of the University of Cincinnati.

He lives in Santa Monica, California.